BBC

A to Z of animal hospital

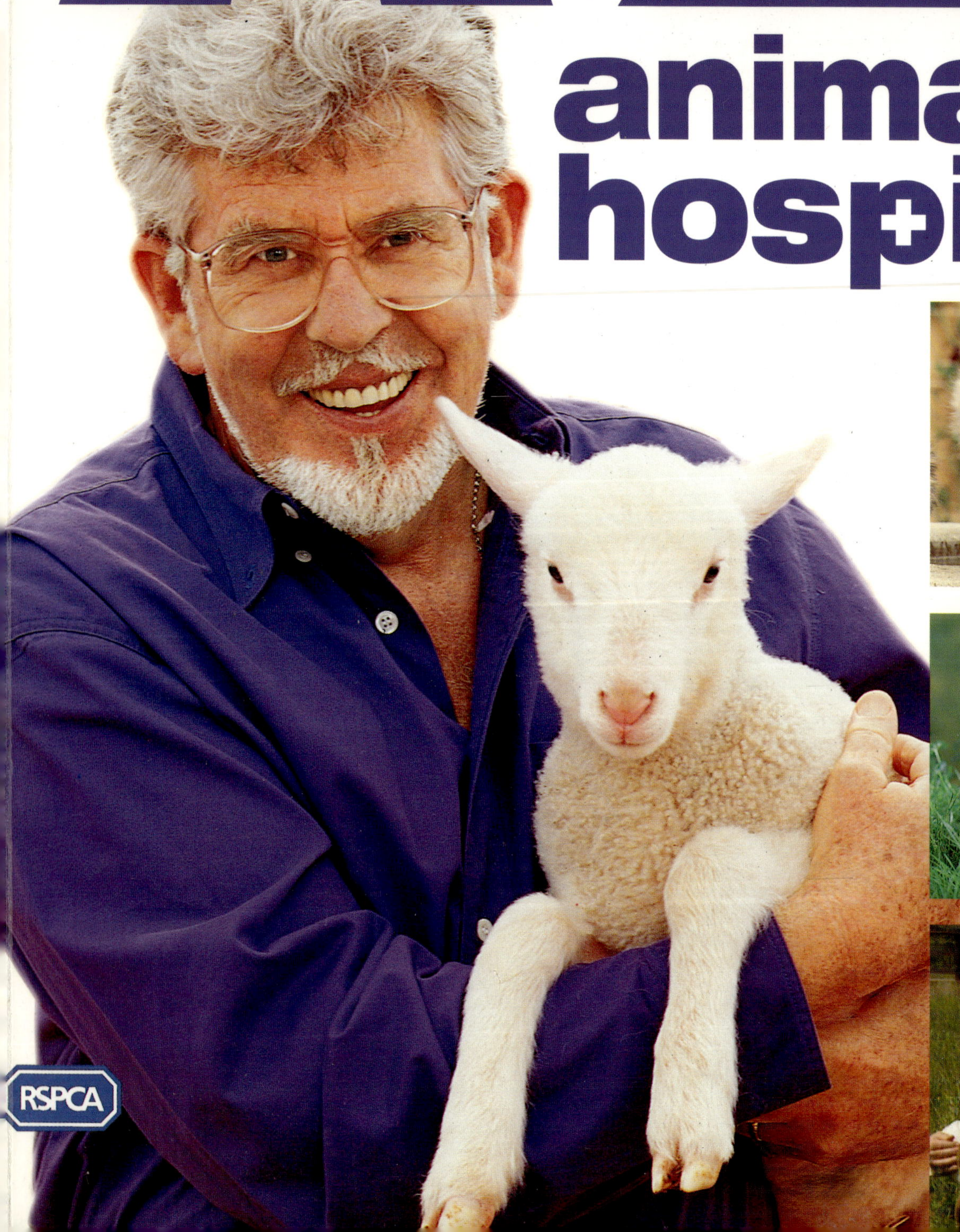

RSPCA

animal hospital

G'day!

Meeting Keiko the Whale on the Animal Hospital Goes West series was one of the highlights of the trip to California.

I've met some great personalities over the years... and their owners! Some pets have had me chuckling with laughter, while others have made me shed tears of sadness but every animal has taught me just how important is the work of the RSPCA, with the vets, the staff and all the other people who care for animals day in and day out.

Animal Hospital has been a wonderful programme to make, not least because of the friends I have made along the way. Don't forget, we have travelled to the United States and Australia to introduce you to some incredible characters and some of the more unusual animals that you wouldn't see walking through the surgery doors at RSPCA Putney or Harmsworth hospitals on an average day.

This book is bursting with pictures and stories that have featured in Animal Hospital, as well as some that we simply haven't had time to show you. So enjoy Animal Hospital as I have seen it, and get an insider's view of the whole range of extraordinary animals and people I have met, right through the alphabet from A to Z.

On the walls of the Harmsworth Animal Hospital waiting room is a mural I painted. This was dedicated to some of the pets we met on the Animal Hospital Goes Live series.

A to Z of... animal hospital

Editor:
Sarah Armstrong-Prior

Art Director:
Helmuth Rautenbach

Cover photograph:
James Jordan

Pictures on pages 2, 4, 6, 8, 9, 10, 13, 15, 16, 17, 20, 27, 30, 32, 43, and 48 supplied by
Bruce Colman

Group Special Projects Editor:
Jaynie Senior

Publisher:
Toni Round

A-Z of Animal Hospital First published in 1999 by BBC Worldwide Limited, 80 Wood Lane, London W12 0TT

ISBN 0 563 55556 4 Text, specially-commissioned photography and design copyright © BBC Worldwide Limited 1999

RSPCA name and logo are trademarks of the RSPCA, licensed by RSPCA Trading Limited. **RSPCA** is a registered charity no. 219099

Animal Hospital is a trademark of the BBC. Animal Hospital logo copyright © BBC

Colour Reproduction by Kestrel Digital Colour, Chelmsford

Printed and bound in Great Britain by Caledonian International Book Manufacturing Limited

TOP: Brave keepers at Corumba examine a young croc... but not without taking precautions first!

RIGHT: Some of the wild birds found in Queensland, Australia.

Many kangaroos have found a home at the Corumban Wildlife Sanctuary.

a is for... AUSTRALIA

The Animal Hospital team was lucky to be able to travel to Rolf's home country, Australia, to visit some of the vets and their patients over there.

The first stop on their tour was the Corumban Wildlife Sanctuary in Queensland, home to over 1,000 birds and animals.

One of the nurses there showed Rolf around the sanctuary.

Their first patient was a female fruit bat who had caught her wing in some barbed wire. Part of the wing needed to be trimmed away to help new tissue to grow.

Next, it was on to the dingo enclosure to meet 'Di', a female dingo who was looking unwell. The vet needed to get close enough to Di to be able to shoot an anaesthetic dart at her.

Once the dingo was unconscious, the vet noticed that Di had a swollen gum. A rotten front tooth and a loose back tooth would both have to be removed.

Fortunately, these were only minor dental problems, and Di would be able to eat normally again by the evening.

Another part of the Animal Hospital tour 'Down Under' that Rolf found extremely exciting, was when he joined a flying vet on his rounds. The vet's name was Graham Stabler, and Rolf caught up with him on his way to check out some poorly cattle at a local ranch.

Drought can be very serious in Australia and can lead to a lot of problems. One of the illnesses that drought can cause is 'tick fever'.

The vet explained to Rolf that when a cow has tick fever, it often appears dopey and wobbly on its legs. If left untreated the cows can even die.

The only way to test for this illness is to check blood samples, so the first step was for the vet to take a sample from each of the cattle.

Vet Graham carried out the tests and treated the cattle with a special injection.

The next flying visit was made to a farm that had reported a horse in trouble. The horse had caught her foot on a barbed wire fence. Vet Graham and Rolf raced to the horse's aid.

Luckily, the mare's wound did not require stitching, so Graham applied a disinfectant spray that would prevent any further bleeding and then bandaged the leg with a secure dressing.

More Australian Adventures

Rolf and the Animal Hospital team also paid visits to kangaroos and their joeys, koalas and ostriches. You can read all about them on pages 23 and 28.

Rolf comforts the worried foal of an injured horse.

Spike, an old male African lion. He needed steroids to help him gain the weight he'd lost because of old age.

AGED ANIMALS

When Animal Hospital followed the work of vets and keepers at Whipsnade Wild Animal Park, we learned of Spike and Dotty, a couple of lions that were having problems related to their age.

The lionkeeper explained that Spike was an elderly male lion whose health had deteriorated over the past week.

Spike was around 20 years old and had recently suffered lots of muscle wastage. Spike's ribs were covered with very thin skin and he needed help from a vet.

The vet prescribed steroids to build Spike up. He then moved Spike and Dotty into a smaller enclosure so the aged pair could get more rest.

Although Dotty was also under the weather, she did not need any treatment. The vet was hopeful that, with rest, Dotty would improve on her own.

Luckily, a week later, Spike and Dotty were much better.

AGE OF HORSES

You really can guess a horse's age from its teeth!

At birth: when a new foal is born, it has just two small milk teeth in each jaw.

One month: a second set of milk teeth appear in each jaw.

Eight months: all the temporary teeth are present – there are six in each jaw. These teeth have small dips or 'cups' in them, which will wear down over time.

Aged 2½: First pair of adult front teeth erupt in each jaw and gradually wear down.

Aged 3½: Second pair of teeth erupt in each jaw.

Aged 4½: Third pair of teeth erupt in each jaw.

Teeth erupt at six, seven and eight years. The cups disappear in the same order as the teeth erupt. Over eight years, a horse is referred to as aged.

AAAH!

All puppies are cute, and although they start off tiny, did you know that some breeds of dog can grow up to weigh a huge 90kg?!

Although male puppies tend to grow bigger than females, you can usually tell roughly how big your puppy will be when adult, especially if you meet its parents.

b is for...

Poor Amber had lost almost all of her hair before receiving treatment at RSPCA Harmsworth.

BALDNESS

Amber the hamster was brought into the RSPCA Animal Hospital clinic because he had suddenly lost all of his hair.

After examining Amber, vet James Yates said the baldness was probably caused by mites, small insects that burrow under the skin to feed.

The owner said that he had recently given Amber a different brand of bedding, which may have carried the mites.

Amber was given an injection to cure the mite infestation. Vet James explained that it would probably take two to three weeks for Amber's hair to grow back.

In the meantime, Amber would have to stay out of the sun, to stop him turning from pink to red!

BATS

Vet Helen Kemp was on duty at the Animal Hospital when an RSPCA officer brought a very angry patient to surgery.

An injured bat had been found on a road and had bitten the poor RSPCA officer who tried to capture it.

The feisty creature now sounded extremely angry and for such a small animal was making a lot of noise.

The RSPCA officer wore special protective gloves as he removed the bat from its container for the vet to examine.

Vet Helen found that its wings were fine, but the bat was rather dehydrated. Dehydration can prevent a bat from flying, so the vet decided to treat it with some glucose water. Using a syringe, Helen carefully fed the bat with the solution.

The RSPCA officer then waited until dusk before he set off to release the bat in the same area where he had found it.

Though the bat was a little reluctant to leave at first, it soon changed its mind and flew off into the night.

The angry bat was fed a high-energy glucose drink through a syringe.

BUDGIE

Joey the Budgie was taken to RSPCA Harmsworth Hospital with a swollen foot. Vet Jeremy Stewart instantly identified the problem. Joey's previous owner had put a ring around her leg, which had imbedded itself into her leg as she grew.

Jeremy tried to remove the ring, but Joey's leg started bleeding. Blood loss in small creatures can be very serious, so the vet needed to cut the ring off and stop the bleeding as soon as possible.

As Jeremy cut into the ring, the bone in Joey's leg crumbled. Jeremy had to make the decision to amputate Joey's leg. After the operation, Joey spent 24 hours in intensive care and was kept on a drip to help rebuild her strength. Courageous Joey eventually made a full recovery and coped well with having only one leg to stand on.

BUDGERIGARS ABOUND!

1) The oldest recorded pet budgie was Charlie, who lived until he was 29.
2) The budgie with the largest vocabulary was Puck, who knew around 1,728 words by the time he died.
3) Budgerigars usually live between five and 10 years.
4) Budgerigars are native to Australia.
5) Budgie chicks weigh a tiny two grams each when they first hatch.

The cause of Duffy's bad breath was a tooth infection that required surgery. Duffy was not amused…

BAD BREATH

Bad breath can be embarrassing for humans, but what happens when it is the pet that has the problem?

RSPCA Animal Hospital vets have seen many cases. In fact, bad breath can often be a symptom of another problem…

The embarrassed owners of Duffy the cat, brought her to the surgery because they could not stand her breath any longer!

Chief vet David Grant examined Duffy's mouth and immediately saw what was causing the problem. Duffy's teeth were in poor condition and she had a small abscess as well.

The vet explained that plaque had built up causing a bacterial infection. The problem had arisen because animals can't clean their teeth like a human does.

Duffy had a severe infection and would need to have some teeth removed.

David administered an antibiotic injection and then gave her an anaesthetic before looking at her teeth.

The infection had cleared up, but some of the loose teeth would need to be removed.

When the vet pulled Duffy's teeth, they came out very easily. He then cleaned and polished her remaining teeth and waited for her to come out of the anaesthetic.

A few hours later, Duffy was still quite sore but seemed much better already.

Duffy made a full recovery and much to her owners' relief, her bad breath had gone.

BUNNIES

Did you know that 'bunnies' is the proper word used to describe baby rabbits?

- The smallest bunny recorded was a new mix of the Netherland Dwarf and the Polish Dwarf. It was bred by a Frenchman in 1975, and weighed just 396g.
- The largest baby bunny was a French female. In 1985, at five months old, she weighed a huge 12kg.

Nola, the Congo Buffalo at Whipsnade, who was bullied after her foot got stuck in a rubber tyre.

BUFFALO AND THE BUGGY

The Animal Hospital team were called in to help handle a buffalo at Whipsnade Wild Animal Park.

A buffalo called Nola had managed to get a baby's buggy tyre caught on her foot.

One of her keepers had succeeded in separating Nola from the rest of the herd but needed help to free her foot.

Buffalo can be quite nasty if they feel threatened and when Nola was let out of her enclosure, the rest of the herd panicked, chased Nola and attacked her.

The keeper explained that because Nola had been isolated from the herd for 12 hours, the buffalo were now suspicious of her.

It took three more keepers to separate a tired and frightened Nola from the rest of the herd again.

But there was some good luck! All that running about had caused the tyre to fall off her leg, actually helping Nola out of her predicament.

Apart from being a little scared, she was safe and uninjured.

Soon Nola was welcomed back by the rest of the herd.

C is for... CRUELTY

Sometimes it is hard to understand why humans behave the way they do, particularly when they are cruel to animals.

In one appalling case, a lady found a dog in very bad condition and took it straight to the nearest police station. The dog was then sent to the Harmsworth.

The poor dog looked pathetic and was in extreme pain. It hardly had a coat of fur at all.

The fur that it did have was terribly matted and so thick around its eyes, the dog could barely see.

When vet Bairbre O'Malley checked the animal's teeth for signs of its age, she could scarcely believe her eyes. He was only a young dog, but looked in such bad condition that he could have been any age.

As the dog's skin was so red and sore, Bairbre decided to sedate it before the examination.

While the dog was asleep, she took a skin scraping to check for a skin disease called mange, and some blood samples for screening. The dog was even scratching in its sleep.

The blood was tested for any signs of internal problems with the liver, kidneys and stomach. The dog was obviously severely malnourished, but it was important to find out whether he had any other medical problems.

While the vet carried out these tests, the RSPCA inspector shot a video of the dog to be used as evidence in a possible court case against the owners.

Bairbre gave the poor creature some food and water to help build it up, and to ease its nerves.

By the next morning, the sweet-tempered dog was already showing signs of improvement.

He was treated for severe malnutrition, but luckily she had no other major problems.

The abandoned dog was in a sorry state. It was thin and its eyes had cataracts.

CANAL DOG

RSPCA officers were called out to a canal bank to rescue a distressed dog that had been dumped there.

From across the water, the RSPCA officer could tell that the dog looked in pretty poor shape and needed to be taken to RSPCA Harmsworth Hospital as soon as possible.

It was not going to be easy. Catching the dog would involve rowing a boat to the far bank where she was stranded and bringing her back across the water in the boat.

At first it didn't look as though the dog was going to co-operate, but with some careful coaxing, the officer soon managed to catch the dog and get her into the boat.

You can report animal cruelty by calling the RSPCA Cruelty Hotline: 0870 5555999

Sadly, this cat did not survive its ordeal, but the RSPCA managed to catch the culprit.

CANAL CAT

Canals and rivers unfortunately make popular dumping spots for unwanted pets, so many incidents involving cruelty arise from these sites. This is where the RSPCA's role can be vital in saving and protecting the lives of defenceless animals.

When the police called the RSPCA to a canal, to rescue a drowning cat, the chance of its survival was slim at best.

The police had been called by a member of the public who had witnessed a man throw the kitten into the water from a bridge.

The young kitten was struggling to stay afloat when the police arrived on the scene in a rescue boat.

The RSPCA officer quickly boarded the boat and went to the cat's rescue. He managed to pull the cat from the water, and tried to revive it.

The kitten was in shock and its heart was racing. It was taken to Harmsworth, but there was little anyone could do for the poor animal. Very sadly, it died soon after.

This was a wicked case of cruelty.

Fortunately, the RSPCA managed to prosecute the kitten's former owner. The defendant pleaded guilty and was punished.

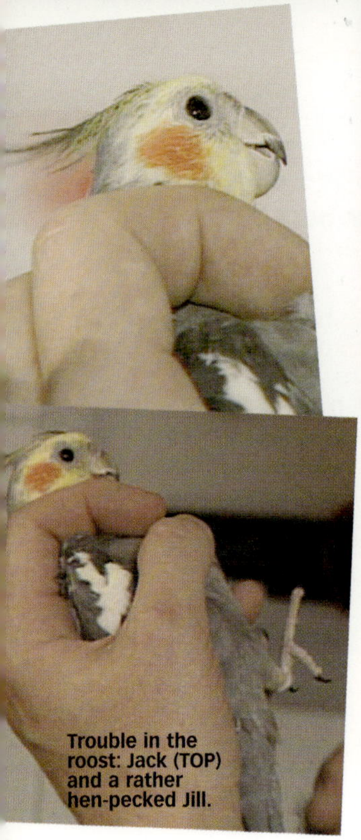

Trouble in the roost: Jack (TOP) and a rather hen-pecked Jill.

COCKATIELS

Jack and Jill were two cockatiels brought into the RSPCA Harmsworth clinic by their owner after some trouble in the roost!

While Jack seemed fine, his cage-mate Jill had gone bald.

The vet thought that it might be a dietary problem but the owner explained that both birds ate well and were fed on the correct foods for cockatiels.

Why was Jill so sore when Jack's feathers were in such good condition? After some more questions, vet Jeremy Stewart hit upon the answer.

Apparently, Jack was a rather feisty bird and wasn't happy about Jill getting attention from their owner.

It looked as though Jack had been pecking Jill, causing her to lose her feathers.

It was also likely that stress had made her baldness even worse.

It was a simple case of bird bullying so, for the vet, the solution was simple too: Separate the two birds!

CAT FACTS

1) Domestic cats can travel at up to 48km per hour.
2) The ancestor of all domestic cats is the African Wild Cat which still exists today.
3) Today, there are around 100 breeds of domestic cat.
4) The domestic cat, which is tame from birth, arose through genetic mutation.
5) Hunting is not always instinctive for cats. Kittens which are born to non-hunting mums may never learn to hunt.
6) The average cat food meal is equivalent to about five mice.
7) Cats have a 'homing device' that uses their biological clock, the angle of the sun and the earth's magnetic field. A cat taken far away from its home can find its way back. However, if a cat's owners move very far away, the cat will not be able to find them.
8) If a male cat has both orange and black fur colouring, it is not only very rare but the cat will also be sterile.
9) A cat has five toes on its front paws, but only four on each back paw.
10) Cats lack a true collarbone, which is why they can usually squeeze their bodies through any hole they can get their head through.

d is for...

DANGER!

Not all animals are cute and cuddly. Many can be quite dangerous. RSPCA staff are all specially trained to deal with potentially dangerous animals.

If you ever come into contact with an animal that you are unsure about, leave it well alone and call in an expert to help.

One evening, the RSPCA received a call from a lady who had fished a box containing an animal out of a nearby canal.

When RSPCA inspector Paul West arrived at the RSPCA Harmsworth later that evening, he brought with him the very unusual cargo.

Inspector Paul West had discovered that the polystyrene box contained an angry rattlesnake.

Vet Helen Kemp advised Paul to telephone London Zoo to see if they were prepared to take the snake. Luckily, the zoo kindly agreed.

The zoo curator struggled to get the snake out of its box. It was nearly 2m long and very heavy. Eventually, the snake began to co-operate and slithered into its new home.

Its bite can take just seven minutes to kill you!

The curator told Paul that the rattlesnake was an Eastern Diamond Back. This type of snake is regarded as America's most venomous. A bite from this poisonous snake can take just seven minutes to kill you!

This particular snake was not even fully grown, short of its potential 3.65m by a long way! The lady who found the snake had been very lucky.

DEER

Road traffic accidents, or RTAs, are a common cause of the injuries that vets at the Harmsworth constantly have to deal with.

Some of the worst accidents are those involving wild animals.

For most wild animals, human contact can over-stress them, especially if they are sick or have been injured. Such stress or shock alone can prove fatal.

In one incident, a Muntjack deer was brought in to see vet Bairbre O'Malley after it had been hit by a car. It was vital that the team handled the deer as carefully as possible to avoid adding further to its trauma.

A female roe deer stands alert in a mixed wood.

To protect the deer, the team worked silently and in semi-darkness. Once the deer had been anaesthetised, Bairbre had a look at its injuries.

A car had hit the deer from behind, seriously damaging its tail. It also had a nasty muscular wound that the vet had to clean and stitch up.

The deer was then transported to a nearby wildlife sanctuary to recover. Within an hour of waking up, the deer was able to stand and even walk around. The vets were pleased with these promising signs.

Fortunately, the deer made such good progress that, after only a few weeks, it was well enough to be returned to its natural habitat in the wild.

Damsel in distress!
This duck was defended for three hours by a passing lady, worried about his health.

DUCK DEFENCE!

How far would you go to help an animal in distress? One determined lady stood guard over a duck that she found on the pavement for three hours before the RSPCA were on the scene.

The lady explained to the arriving officer that she had found the duck looking quite lost in the middle of the pavement.

Afraid that it might be attacked by dogs or cats, she had stood guard while her husband went off to get help.

The duck seemed unable to stretch one of its wings properly.

The RSPCA officer on the scene used a net to catch the duck, which was reluctant to be caught and put up quite a struggle.

The duck was then taken back to the RSPCA Harmsworth to be examined by chief vet David Grant.

Once inside, the duck became quite fierce and seemed to have plenty of energy.

David checked the duck for broken bones but found none. He noted that the duck was well fed and seemed in good condition.

Fortunately, he was able to give the duck a clean bill of health and explained that it was a young male and had probably just got lost.

The duck was kept in for a day for observation and then released in a safe area, where it was able to fly off with no problem at all.

DO YOU KNOW DOGS?

1) The heaviest and longest recorded dog was an Old English Mastiff called Zorba. In 1989, Zorba was 2.53 metres long from nose to tail. He weighed a huge 156 kg.

2) The world's oldest dog reliably recorded was an Australian cattle dog named Bluey, who was put to sleep aged 29 years and five months old.

3) The world's smallest dog was the size of a matchbox! At two years old and fully-grown, the tiny Yorkie from Blackburn, England, was an incredible 11.4 cm long and 7.6 cm tall.

4) The tallest recorded dog was called 'Shamgret Danzas'. The dog was 1.28 metres tall at the shoulder and weighed 108 kg.

5) The Dachshund is one of the oldest dog breeds in history, dating back to ancient Egyptian times.

6) The Bloodhound is the only animal whose evidence has been considered admissible (allowed) in an American court of law.

7) Dogs only have about 10 vocal sounds, whereas cats have around 100.

8) The richest dog in the world today is probably a German Shepherd called 'Gunther'. When his countess owner died, he was left around £40 million in her will.

9) The highest jump made by a dog was recorded in 1993 in Gloucestershire, England. 'Stag', an 18-month-old lurcher, set the record with a 3.72 metre leap.

e is for... EMERGENCY!

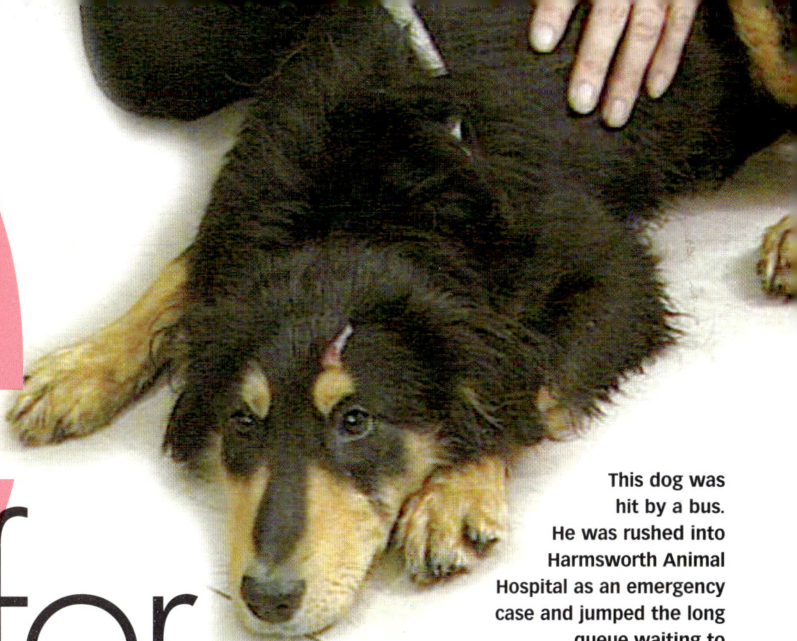

This dog was hit by a bus. He was rushed into Harmsworth Animal Hospital as an emergency case and jumped the long queue waiting to see the vet.

The surgery at RSPCA's Harmsworth Animal Hospital is always busy and there is often a long waiting list to see the vet. However, when an emergency comes in, it automatically jumps the queue.

In one such case, a dog was brought in by two dog wardens who, luckily, had been on the scene when the dog was hit by a bus.

Road traffic accidents are unfortunately very common and can often be fatal.

Vet Bairbre O' Malley was on duty when the dog was brought in. It had taken the dog wardens 15 minutes to reach the Harmsworth because of the traffic, so immediate veterinary attention could have proved vital.

Although the dog seemed fine, delayed shock is common in such cases, and shock can itself be fatal. Bairbre was keen to give the dog a thorough check before deciding on a course of action.

She noticed the dog was walking with a limp, which may have been from bruising received on impact with the bus, or perhaps something more serious.

After examining the dog, the vet established that there were no broken bones. It looked as though the hardy dog had escaped with just bruising.

However, the dog could still go into shock, so Bairbre decided to admit him for observation, putting him on a drip to help prevent shock development.

After nurses had administered some antibiotics and painkillers, the dog was left to rest. It was now a case of wait-and-see.

Luckily, after a few hours, the dog seemed fine. The vet explained that she would still keep him in overnight for observation.

The following morning, it was clear that the dog was fit to leave, so the RSPCA took him off to Battersea Dogs' Home where they could begin the search for his owner.

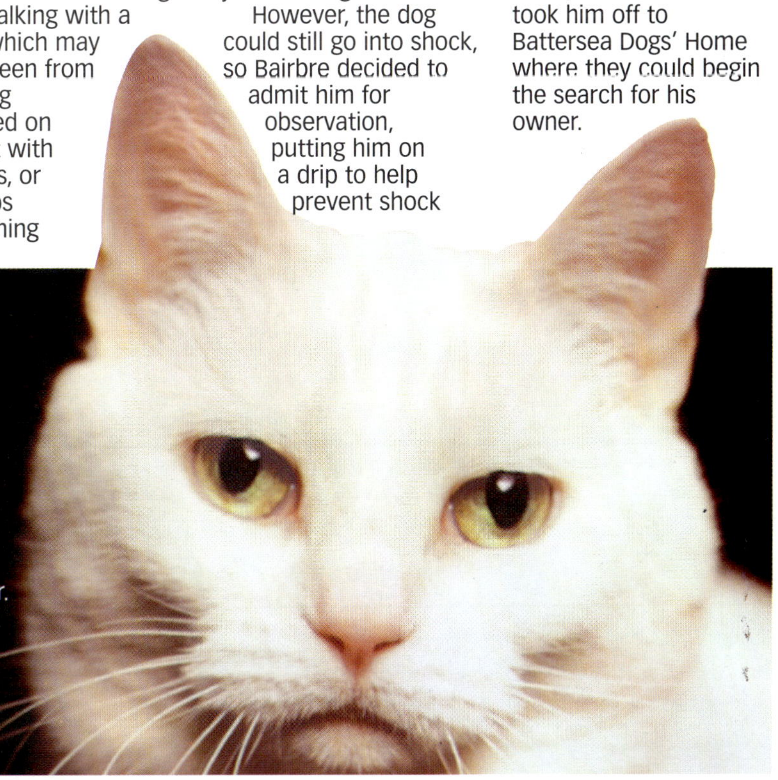

EARS AND EYES

- **Cats' eyes are adapted for hunting.** They can see best in dim light just before dawn and just after dusk.
- **The biggest-eared bunny recorded was 'Toby II',** an English lop-eared bunny whose ears were 74.3 cm long and 18.7 cm wide!
- **Unlike all other rodents,** guinea pigs can see in colour.
- **Horses have the largest eyes of all land mammals.** They also have brilliant eyesight.
- **Dogs are not colour blind.**

Salamander: an unusual pet rescued by the RSPCA.

Exotic pets are quite rare in this country, and require a great deal of specialist care. Many owners cannot provide the right conditions for their pets to stay healthy.

EXOTIC: SALAMANDER

A startled lady called the RSPCA when she found a stray salamander in her back garden.

A salamander is a tropical amphibian, normally found abroad, so it must have been an escaped pet.

The RSPCA inspector captured the exotic animal and noticed that its back legs were injured. He also noticed puncture wounds on either side of the salamander's pelvis. The inspector took it to Harmsworth where it was examined by a very surprised vet Gabriel Haggard.

Vet Gabriel said that the salamander had probably been attacked by a puzzled cat or dog. The infected wounds had made its back legs rather painful.

The vet did not want to damage the delicate skin of the amphibian with an antibiotics injection, so he used a syringe to spray antibiotics directly onto the wounds themselves.

exotic pets

Here are three true stories involving exotic pets...

EXOTIC: PYTHON

Vet Liz Forbes was on duty when Dick, a 4.6m long python, weighing a massive 38 kilos, was carried into the RSPCA's Putney Animal Hospital surgery.

The python's owner told the vet that Dick was normally a very playful pet!

Lately, however, he had been a bit 'snuffly' and would not allow anyone near his face.

Dick's owner thought he might have a cold. He was still eating well, but had quite noticeable breathing difficulties.

Liz asked about the python's living conditions, and learnt that he lived in a vivarium that was only around 1.8m by 1.8m.

This was not nearly big enough for such a large reptile.

Moreover, at only three years old, Dick was likely to grow even bigger still.

Liz explained to the owner that Dick would need a larger vivarium as soon as possible.

Dick's respiratory problems were probably due to stress caused by his cramped living conditions.

Liz treated the python with an antibiotic injection and told the owner to buy Dick a new vivarium.

Hopefully, a bigger home would put a swift end to the poorly python's problem.

It took three grown men to get this patient into the sugery.

Reggie – hungry again!

EXOTIC: PIRANHAS!

RSPCA chief inspector Ian Gough didn't know quite what to expect when he was called by one worried pet owner who couldn't cope with his pets 'Ronnie and Reggie'.

The owner explained that about a month ago, a friend had given him a pair of piranhas. However, this friend had not been totally honest, neglecting to mention their size.

Moreover, he was unsure whether the piranhas were of the flesh-eating variety or not. The owner explained that he had been feeding Ronnie and Reggie with ham, sausages and bacon.

The owner explained that he had been feeding Ronnie and Reggie with ham, sausages and bacon.

The RSPCA officer explained that the piranhas may have been eating this food because it was the only food available to them.

The Eagle Heights sanctuary agreed to take in the pair of piranhas. The plan was to transport Ronnie and Reggie to their new home in separate dustbins. Inspector Ian placed each piranha in a strong plastic bag filled with water before inserting the bag inside a bin.

The inspector had to be careful not to get his hands near the pair, and so used a long net to capture them. The reluctant fish splashed about quite a bit.

At Eagle Heights, Ronnie and Reggie were released into their new tanks. Their carer confirmed that they were indeed meat-eating, red-bellied piranhas! Ian's precautions had not been in vain!

EWES AND LAMBS

1) 'Ewe' is the correct name for female adult sheep. 'Lamb' is the term used for infants.
2) Lambs usually learn to stand only hours after birth.
3) It is important that newborn lambs drink the ewe's milk within 12 hours of birth. The milk contains colostrum, which passes on vital nutrients, as well as passing on immunity to certain diseases.
4) At least two of the most popular English nursery rhymes refer to lambs and sheep.
5) In literature, lambs are often used to represent something good, pure and innocent.

f is for...

FISH

Fish go to the vet too! As the Animal Hospital team discovered when they visited a private vet in Aylesbury.

When the Animal Hospital team caught up with the staff at Hampden Veterinary Hospital, they met an owner who had brought in his pet carp to see vet Malcolm Paul.

The fish had previously suffered from pox that affected its fins. This had now cleared up, but the large dorsal fin on its back was bright pink and looked extremely painful.

Malcolm explained that the fish had an infection called septicaemia. The pink fin was a symptom of this.

Vet Malcolm injected some antibiotics into the muscle on the carp's back. He had to be very careful not to damage the delicate fish scales. After getting thoroughly soaked, the vet was able to reassure the man that his pet carp would soon be feeling better.

Long-haired cats require regular grooming.

FUR AND GROOMING

Fur acts in the same way as clothes do for humans. Fur helps to protect the animal's skin and keeps it warm or cool.

All dogs need regular grooming. How much they need depends on the type of coat.

Grooming improves the appearance of short-coated varieties. For long-haired and curly-haired dogs, it is essential.

The same rule applies for cats, although they are good at grooming and cleaning themselves.

Remember that long-haired rabbits, guinea pigs and hamsters also need regular grooming!

FOX

One poor fox was found in a terrible fix! Workers at a warehouse were mystified when the intruder alarm kept going off. Then one of the warehouse workers spotted the culprit – a fox.

The RSPCA officer on the scene decided to capture the fox using food as bait. It took two days to catch the wily fox.

He checked for any injuries but the fox seemed in good health, so he decided to release it back into the wild as soon as possible.

The officer found a nearby park that provided the perfect place for the fox to find its feet again. Then, he let his captive go and watched it scuttle off into the park bushes.

Sleeping beauty! A fox takes an early morning nap on a disused farm building.

FAWN

While the Animal Hospital team were following the work of vets and keepers at Whipsnade Wild Animal Park, they came across a baby Chinese Water Deer that needed help...

Lucy and her keeper.

Rolf soon made friends with Lucy, the orphaned fawn who was hand-reared at Whipsnade.

The keepers at Whipsnade Wild Animal Park had received reports that an orphaned fawn called Lucy had been attacked by a crow. Her head was badly pecked and needed to be cleaned up, stitched and dressed by a vet.

The wounds would take quite a while to heal and, because she was so young, Lucy would need hand-rearing during this time.

After being in contact with humans, Lucy would need to be slowly re-introduced to the herd, otherwise they would reject her.

Lucy was bottle-fed for a couple of weeks and her keepers were delighted to see her making great progress.

She was soon well enough to start being introduced to the whole stable of deer and eventually she would be able to roam freely with the rest of the deer herd at Whipsnade.

Guinea pigs make great pets as they are fairly easy to look after. They are also adorably cute — like this one!

GUINEA PIG

Bump the guinea pig was brought in to see vet Bairbre O' Malley by his worried owner.

Bump had lost a lot of weight and had become very inactive.

His owner said Bump was always fed on dried food made especially for guinea pigs.

Bairbre examined Bump and said that he was suffering from a vitamin deficiency, a common problem in guinea pigs.

She told the owner to change Bump's diet so it consisted mainly of fresh greens and fruit.

Bump would also need to have some vitamin C tablets dissolved in his drinking water.

In the meantime, Bairbre gave the guinea pig a vitamin C injection to initiate his recovery.

GERBILS AND GUINEA PIGS

1) Gerbils hardly ever squeak unless they are frightened or fighting.
2) The largest ever litter of guinea pigs was twelve, recorded in 1972.
3) Gerbils normally live for three to four years.
4) Both humans and guinea pigs can develop a skin complaint called 'scurvy', caused by a vitamin C deficiency.
5) Just like rabbits, guinea pigs eat their droppings to gain all the nutrients from their food.

g is for... GOOSE

One cheeky pet proved quite a challenge for Hampden Hospital's chief vet Colin Price.

The cheeky pet was a goose called Daisy. Her owner explained that although she had been enjoying her food, Daisy had lost weight and seemed depressed and moody.

Moreover, Daisy had not laid a single egg for five days.

The usually good-tempered goose was also aggressive when vet Colin tried to examine her.

Colin explained that she had probably stopped laying eggs to conserve her energy, because she did seem a little thin.

The problem became more obvious when Colin asked Daisy's owner when she had last wormed Daisy.

Her owner had not realised that geese, just like cats and dogs, need to be regularly wormed. This was likely to be the main cause of Daisy's weight loss.

The vet gave the lady a special wormer that she could pop into Daisy's food.

Daisy's owner reported that, after just a few days, Daisy had already put on weight.

Daisy virtually had the run of the house, but Shauna soon had the goose eating out of her hand!

h is for...

HAMSTERS

- Hamsters are very active when awake and can travel as far as 20 kilometres in one night.
- The largest litter of pet hamsters was 26, recorded in 1974.
- Dwarf hamsters can communicate with each other by making ultrasonic squeaks that humans cannot hear.
- All hamsters in captivity today are descendants of a single family found in Syria in 1932.
- Hamsters have successfully mated at as young as four weeks old.

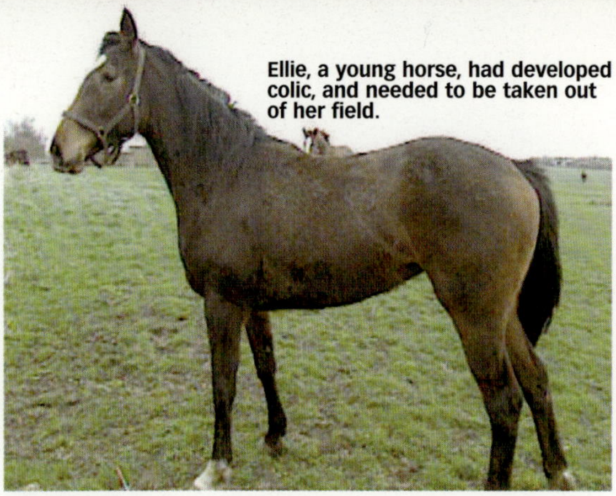

Ellie, a young horse, had developed colic, and needed to be taken out of her field.

HORSE

Colic is a common illness in horses, but it can be fatal in a matter of hours. If it is not spotted early enough, it can result in a build-up of gas in the stomach and can lead to a twisted gut. As colic can be so serious, it needs veterinary attention as soon as possible.

When the Animal Hospital team were following the staff of the private Hampden Hospital in Aylesbury, a horse called Ellie developed colic and needed help from the veterinary team. She was taken out of her field and put in a stable filled with extra hay for padding.

When vet Ian Baker arrived, he listened to Ellie's stomach to see how bad the problem was. He could hear no gut sounds at all, which can sometimes be a very bad sign.

The vet gave Ellie an antispasmodic injection to ease the pain. Ian examined Ellie's gut to check that it was not twisted, but there was little more he could do. Now they would have to wait.

Amazingly, Ellie's colic passed quickly and she was soon returned to her field. However, as colic can be life threatening, Ellie's owner had been right to call the vet immediately.

HEDGEHOG

A tiny hedgehog was brought into the Harmsworth by an RSPCA driver who had spotted him in a garden with maggots crawling around his eyes.

Maggots can cause worms, so duty nurse Francis had to clean them off as soon as possible.

As she did so, she noticed that the hedgehog also had a flea infestation, which she treated with a special flea spray suitable for such young hedgehogs.

As the hedgehog weighed only 85g, he was too small to be released back into the wild, so he would have to be hand-reared until he was the correct weight. Nurse Francis volunteered to take the baby hedgehog home. She named him Dominic.

Within four weeks, Dominic's weight had soared to 575g, which meant he was large enough to be let back into the wild.

Dominic was taken home by nurse Francis, who hand-reared him until he was strong enough to return to the wild.

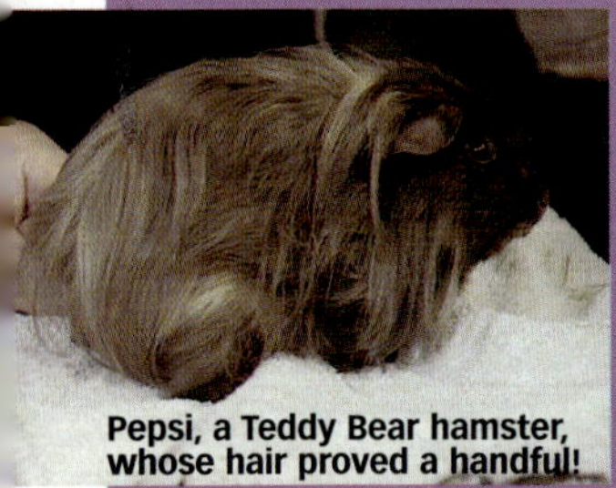

Pepsi, a Teddy Bear hamster, whose hair proved a handful!

HAIRY HAMSTER

Vet Bairbre O'Malley was on duty at the Harmsworth when Pepsi, a very hairy hamster, was brought into surgery.

The reason Pepsi was so hairy was because the hamster was a Teddy Bear hamster, which is an unusual breed in this country renowned for its long hair.

Pepsi's coat was very matted which meant the hamster was having trouble grooming itself properly. Bairbre told Pepsi's owner that she should groom him daily.

Vet Bairbre suggested using a soft toothbrush for this.

She showed Pepsi's owner how to brush the hamster carefully, paying particular attention to any painful knots.

Once Bairbre had finished, Pepsi looked much more comfortable and even cuter than he did before!

George seemed moody, so his owner took him to the vet to see if he could find out what was troubling the hawk.

HARRIS HAWK

George the Harris Hawk was brought into the Hampden surgery by his owner because he had noted a change in George's behaviour.

George had become moody and had also lost his appetite. His owner had stopped flying the hawk to help him conserve his energy.

Vet Malcolm Paul took a general look at the hawk. He listened to his heart and lungs, which sounded fine, and felt the bird's breast muscles to see if he was too thin.

Vet Malcolm said that George felt slightly underweight so he checked for worms.

Luckily, George was given the all-clear. He was merely feeling under-the-weather.

Within a few days, George regained his healthy appetite and was able to fly again.

Actress Tippi Hedren told Rolf that one of the reasons she set up her animal reserve was because she couldn't bear to part with the animals she had starred with in her films.

i is for... INCREDIBLE INDIVIDUAL

When Rolf toured California in the Animal Hospital Goes West series, he met some dedicated individuals who were doing huge amounts to help animals.

This tiger will have a home at Shambala for the rest of its days.

One such lady is Tippi Hedren, the mother of actress Melanie Griffith, who showed Rolf around her sanctuary for big cats.

Shambala Preserve is a sanctuary for around seventy big cats, and a few elephants too. Among the lions, panthers, tigers and other big cats that Rolf observed was a female cheetah with only three legs.

The cheetah had lost one of its hind legs, which meant it would not survive in the wild, but was protected at Shambala where it was also being taught to cope with its disability.

The cheetah's carer explained that even on three legs the cheetah could run at an incredible 56km/h.

Tippi and Rolf then met Zeus, a male mountain lion who had been brought to Shambala because he had lost his home.

Zeus's carer had made the 22-hour journey to the sanctuary with the lion. She was very upset at having to part with her friend Zeus.

However, she explained that had it not been for Shambala providing the lion with a home, she would have had to put Zeus to sleep.

Previously, Zeus had been allowed to live on a large, private estate. However, the owner had put the land up for sale, which meant Zeus had become homeless.

Tippi then told Rolf that Zeus would have to stay in quarantine for a month before being moved into a large enclosure where he could join some of the other animals.

The rescued three-legged cheetah that Rolf met at Shambala.

ITCHY

Itching is a common sign of parasites.

Remember to de-flea your pet cat or dog (and its bedding) regularly – even if you don't think they have any.

Other parasites include ticks, mites and lice, which can all cause your pet problems, and are easily transferred between animals.

There are many treatments available for all of these conditions, but your vet will be able to advise you which one is best for your pet.

ITCHY DOG

The RSPCA Animal Hospital vets are used to pets with itchy coats.

Among the common causes of itching are fleas, mites and ticks.

However, many of the complaints that the RSPCA Animal Hospital vets see every week are more similar to problems found in humans, as was the case with a boxer dog called Tyke.

Tyke was brought in to see vet Bairbre O'Malley when his owner noticed him scratching his chin.

Tyke's owner had seen some small spots on his chin that sometimes bled.

Bairbre examined Tyke's spotty chin and explained that he had a mild inflammation of his hair follicles. This bacterial infection was similar to the acne that some teenagers get.

In order to treat Tyke's itch, the vet prescribed an antibacterial face wash and a long course of antibiotics.

She showed Tyke's owner how to give the dog's chin a good scrub with the face wash. Tyke would have to be washed daily at first, then around three times a week afterwards.

Hopefully, as Tyke got older, his acne would clear up and his itch would gradually disappear.

IGUANA

Elmo the iguana's young owner was worried about his weight. She thought he might be getting too fat.

Hampden Hospital vet Malcolm Paul examined Elmo and noted that his mouth looked pink and healthy and Elmo was shedding his skin without any problems. He seemed healthy enough.

As Malcolm examined Elmo, he rested his finger on a small opening on top of his head. Apparently, this opening is something all iguanas possess – a third eye!

Malcolm explained to Elmo's owner that covering the third eye helped to calm the iguana, as the eye acts like a body clock – so in darkness, the body naturally thinks it is time to sleep.

Elmo was only about twelve months old, so his weight gain was probably related to growth. His owner had been needlessly worried in this case.

Elmo the iguana.

Not the cuddliest pet in the world!

J is for...

JOKERS

The keepers at Whipsnade had quite a job on their hands when they tried to catch six wolf cubs.

One of the keepers explained that for the first few weeks of their life, wolf cubs stay underground in the safety of the den.

Once the cubs start to come up above ground, they need to be caught so their sex can be determined, and be wormed and microchipped for identification purposes.

The keepers had to locate all six cubs while keeping a very careful eye on the 12 adult wolves.

The situation was potentially quite dangerous. Some of the adults were lurking underground so the keepers had to be very careful.

Unfortunately, the ground was too hard to dig up which made getting at the cubs impossible.

After a long hunt, the keepers decided to come back another day. Good luck!

Peek a boo!! This joker was hiding six cubs somewhere in the underground den.

JAWS

When an animal has a problem with its teeth or jaw, it is the vet's job to act as dentist.

Vet Stan McAsky was on duty when a cat in need of some delicate dentistry arrived at RSPCA's Harmsworth.

Charlie the cat had been injured when he slipped on some concrete steps and fell on his face. In shock, Charlie had run off and hidden for 12 hours.

When he came back home, his owners could see that one of his front teeth was sticking out at a strange angle.

Vet Stan carefully examined Charlie's mouth. The gum beneath Charlie's injured tooth was sore and starting to become infected.

He gave Charlie some antibiotics and an anaesthetic. However, Stan found more than just a broken tooth, Charlie had also fractured part of his lower jaw.

Luckily for Charlie, one stitch through the gum was enough to hold the broken bone in place and, although it would be sore for a while, it would heal eventually.

In fact, later that day, a brave and hungry Charlie had no trouble gobbling up his evening meal!

Charlie's broken tooth would obviously have to come out, but his problem didn't end there.

K is for...

Jack's eye operation went well: he was soon looking and seeing better.

KITTEN

When vet Jeremy Stewart examined a poorly white kitten called Jack, he discovered an unusual deformity which could cause Jack to go blind...

Vet Jeremy Stewart examined Jack's eye and found that Jack had been born with an eye deformity.

The lower lid had an excessive amount of skin tissue, which had made the lid turn in on itself and made the lashes grow in towards the eye.

Jack would need an operation to correct the problem.

Jack's owner said that she thought the kitten was also completely deaf, which Vet Jeremy soon found out to be the case.

A few days later, Jack was anaesthetised for his eye operation.

Very carefully, Jeremy removed the kitten's excess skin with a scalpel before using ten tiny stitches to sew it into position so the lid sat more comfortably.

Within a few hours, Jack was back on the ward at Harmsworth and feeling better.

Fortunately for Jack, the operation was a complete success, and Jack can now see perfectly well through both eyes.

Rocky the Rottweiler's bark was fortunately worse than his bite.

KENNEL COUGH

Kennel cough is a serious illness that may be prevented by vaccination.

Chief vet David Grant was on duty at the Harmsworth Animal Hospital when Rocky, a large Rottweiler, was brought into surgery because he had developed a nasty cough.

David was very careful when examining the twelve-stone dog. Rocky was six years old and still getting bigger!

David explained that dogs should always be handled with respect.

You should never look directly into their eyes, as this can be viewed as a threat.

His owner said Rocky had been ill for nearly two weeks and that each cough was finished with an unpleasant-sounding spit.

David listened to Rocky's heartbeat, which sounded a little fast and irregular.

Next, he very carefully examined the dog's eyes and mouth to check for other symptoms.

He suspected the problem was due to kennel cough, telling Rocky's owner that if his cough did not clear up within seven to 10 days, he should bring Rocky back in.

The following week, Rocky and his owner did not return and we were relieved to learn that Rocky was back to his normal self.

KANGAROOS

It was feeding time when Rolf and the rest of the Animal Hospital team were shown around the kangaroo enclosure at Corumban Wildlife Sanctuary in Queensland, Australia.

There were lots of kangaroos housed at the sanctuary, due to the great numbers injured each year in road accidents.

Rolf was taken to the kangaroo surgery, where a kangaroo was having some stitches removed. She had needed the stitches because her infant joey had torn her pouch. As soon as she awoke, she was ready to be returned to her friends.

An orphaned joey makes himself at home in his make-shift pouch.

KOALAS

Australia's koala population is in trouble. The eucalyptus trees that provide their food are being cut down to make way for modern buildings.

As a result, the Corumban Wildlife Sanctuary houses lots of young koalas who have been orphaned or separated from their families and are unable to fend for themselves.

One koala the Animal Hospital team got to know was Mel, a young female koala that was ready to be released back into the wild.

Mel had been very stressed and emaciated, with bad conjunctivitis in one eye, when she had arrived, 10 months ago.

Poor Mel had such a bad infection, some of her eyelid had needed to be removed.

Almost a year on, Mel was now fit and ready to return home to the wild.

It would be a big step returning to the bush, so her keepers would make Mel's return to the wild a gradual one.

She could always return to the sanctuary if she wanted to.

Mel eventually made her big leap. She got to know her surroundings, and within a few weeks she felt confident enough to leave the sanctuary.

L is for...

LIZARD

Exotic pets need specialist care and attention. Even if you have all the right equipment, they are still very difficult pets to look after and it is not advised that anyone should buy one without serious thought first.

Hector was a Bask Monitor Lizard who was brought into the RSPCA Putney Animal Hospital to see the chief vet Tessa Bailey.

Although this exotic pet's owner had used a special heating mat, there had been a serious problem with it that sadly led to the lizard's death.

When Tessa saw Hector, he was very emaciated and weak, and could hardly walk.

Hector had horrific burns on his tummy, which were possibly from a heating pad.

He also showed some signs of spine curvature.

Tessa examined the burns on Hector's delicate skin, but was also very worried about his spine.

In order to see if there were any broken bones, she took an x-ray. Luckily, no bones were broken. Hector's severe burns needed treatment and Tessa was worried about his chances of recovery.

To increase Hector's body temperature and to help rehydrate him, the lizard was given a warm bath.

Hector would need regular bathing in an iodine solution to help heal his burns and stop them from becoming infected.

Unfortunately, despite Tessa's efforts, Hector died shortly after being admitted to the hospital.

His wounds had already become infected, causing fatal blood poisoning.

LIONS

It is not always obvious whether or not an animal needs help. The RSPCA tries hard to determine whether a call out needs action. It is, however, usually considered better to be safe than sorry.

On one occasion, the RSPCA received a call about some lions being used in a show in London. A member of the public had been anxious about their welfare.

The inspector who answered the call went to investigate the conservation organisation that was using the lions as part of a presentation to raise money.

The lions were only four months old, but they were strong and playful.

The inspector examined the area where the lions were being kept and asked a variety of questions designed to give her clues about the standard of their care.

Having watched them play and interact with their handlers, she was satisfied they were being properly cared for.

LUCKY

One kitten, Lucky, was found by her adopted owner trembling in a graveyard on Halloween.

The kitten's owner explained to vet Bairbre O'Malley that every time Lucky tried to eat, she coughed and brought her food back up.

Bairbre's examination revealed that Lucky had a deformity similar to a cleft palate. She explained that the flap of tissue between the kitten's airway and throat was torn.

This tissue normally divides food from the airway, but the tear meant that it was not doing its job properly. It was a very serious abnormality that needed immediate surgery so Lucky could eat properly and survive.

Lucky lived up to her name, and was eating properly and much happier within two days of her tricky operation.

m is for...

Polo was given an Elizabethan collar to wear to help put an end to her mischief.

MISCHIEF

The RSPCA Animal Hospitals see many pets whose injuries are a result of the pet's own mischievous behaviour. Polo, the cat with a hole, was one such case.

Vet Gabriel Haggard was on duty at the RSPCA Harmsworth when Polo, a feisty cat was brought in.

Her owner explained that Polo kept getting into fights with dogs. Polo's tummy had been injured in her most recent fight.

As soon as Polo's owner was out of sight, Polo began spitting and snarling at Gabriel as he tried to examine her.

He wrapped Polo in a towel to stop her from scratching him while he gave her an injection to sedate her.

Once Polo was heavily sedated, Gabriel discovered two holes that looked like puncture wounds from a dog's bite.

He cleaned the wounds and applied a dressing. However, as the wounds were quite deep, they would need to be stitched up the next day.

While Polo was still anaesthetised, Gabriel decided to take a few precautionary measures.

He bound up her claws and fitted her with a special 'Elizabethan collar' so she wouldn't be so vicious next time she was handled.

The following day, Gabriel managed to give Polo another injection and stitched up her battle wounds.

When Polo awoke, her happy owner came to collect the mischievous cat, who behaved like an angel!

MITES

Many pets can suffer from mites, small parasitic insects that burrow into the animal's skin to feed off its blood.

One of the more unusual cases of mite infestation to arrive at the Harmsworth was that of Satan the iguana.

Satan was a large iguana with a bad skin complaint. His owner said he suspected that Satan had a mite infestation.

The vet examined Satan's skin, which looked very sore. He took a skin scrape to test for these parasites.

Under the microscope, red mites could be seen on the slide. To treat Satan's problem, the vet gave the iguana an injection under his foreleg.

MOUSE

Vet Jeremy Stewart was on duty at the Harmsworth when an RSPCA Inspector brought in a mouse he had rescued from a filthy, broken glass tank.

The mouse's skin had several wounds that were forming scabs, and she looked underweight. She was panting quite heavily and was obviously very distressed. She had lost most of her fur and was scratching herself a lot, indicating a bad parasite problem.

Vet Jeremy was very worried about the mouse. He decided it would be better to let her rest for a day before he attempted to examine her more closely.

When Jeremy examined the mouse a day later, he discovered a mite infestation.

He treated her with a very strong insecticide injection that would need to be repeated in ten days time. He also put her on a special diet.

Within a week, the mouse had already made good progress.

Josie's calf takes a careful look around her new home for the first time.

MOTHER

The atmosphere in the giraffe section of Whipsnade was buzzing when Animal Hospital visited. The keeper explained that one of the giraffes was due to give birth.

Throughout the night, the keeper made regular checks on Josie, the expectant mother.

Giraffes normally give birth to their young under cover of night, but by the next morning, there was still no sign that Josie was ready to go into labour.

A few days later however, Josie chose the middle of the afternoon to give birth.

Unfortunately, she was standing in the enclosure yard, which had hard ground, making it a less than ideal place to give birth.

Josie seemed happy though and the birth went smoothly. Josie had regular contractions, and as the calf dropped to the ground, she licked it.

Soon the calf was trying to stand up, but it couldn't quite untangle its long legs and fell back to the ground.

Soon the calf was trying to stand up, but it couldn't untangle its long legs and fell back to the ground.

The keepers decided to carry the calf indoors where the straw-covered floor was softer and warmer.

Within half an hour of the calf's birth, it was able to stand up. Mother and baby were both doing well.

The next morning, it was apparent that the baby giraffe had made excellent progress overnight.

The calf had been spotted suckling in the early hours of the morning, which the keeper said was very good news.

He was pleased that the giraffe was drinking the colostrum-rich milk.

Colostrum is packed with nutrients and antibodies passed on from the mother to the infant, giving immunity and protecting the calf from a number of nasty illnesses.

MICROCHIPPING

- One of the best ways to ensure that you find your pet if it goes missing is to have a microchip implanted.
- A vet can implant a microchip painlessly under the animal's skin.
- This chip contains a unique code that can be read by a special scanner passed over the pet.
- The code is entered into the national PetLog database, which means the pet's details will be registered and its owner can be contacted if the pet gets lost.

Versace the hamster had a mystery object in his right eye that was making it sore.

MYSTERIOUS

Versace the hamster had developed a sore eye and was losing weight and hair.

Versace's worried owner brought him into the Harmsworth clinic.

Vet Gabriel Haggard explained that in hamster terms, four-year-old Versace was getting on a bit.

Hamsters normally live only two or three years and Versace's hair and weight loss were simply symptoms of old age.

Old age did not, however, explain the mysterious problem with Versace's eye.

The vet examined the hamster's eye carefully and spotted a foreign body, which looked like a piece of old food.

As soon as Gabriel had removed the object from Versace's eye, it stopped watering and the mouse seemed to cheer up.

Gabriel gave Versace an injection of antibiotics to combat the eye infection. Soon after, Versace's eye made a full recovery.

n is for...

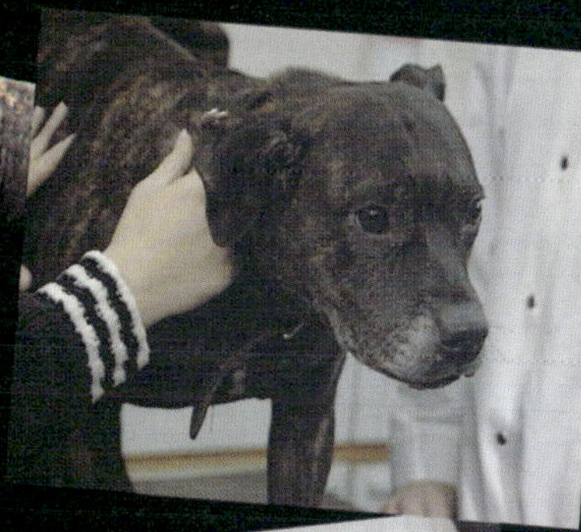

Lady, the naughty Staffie who scoffed a box of chocolates — and their wrappers!

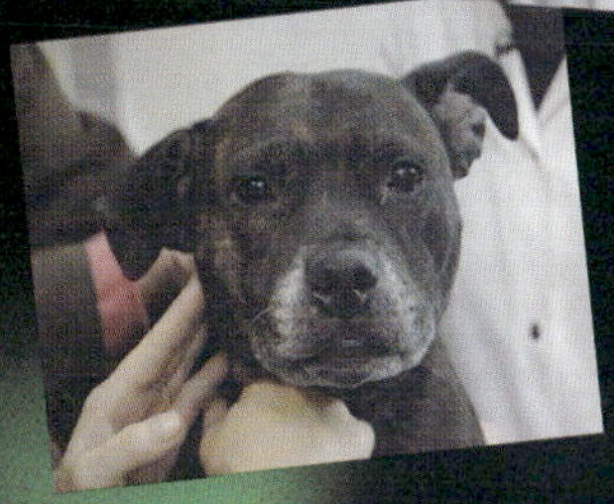

NUTTY SQUIRREL

When RSPCA ambulance driver Jo Cotton was called to King's Cross Station in London, she wasn't sure what to expect!

Customers at a newsagent's had reported a squirrel on the loose that was now hiding in the bookshelves.

When the ambulance driver arrived, quite a crowd had gathered to see what would happen to the literary-minded animal.

A shop assistant led Jo to where the squirrel had been spotted, but Jo was going to need help to catch the squirrel, as she soon found out. She enlisted the help of the shop supervisor.

The plan was for Jo to flush the squirrel out from behind the books and lead it straight to the supervisor, who was standing by with a net.

As a sensible precaution, Jo was wearing thick, protective gloves. She was particularly wary of squirrels, having been bitten by one before.

They chased the squirrel up and down the bookshelves for nearly an hour before Jo finally managed to catch it and put it safely in a box.

The squirrel's rather nutty behaviour suggested that it was in fact fine (though perhaps a little bit lost). The RSPCA officer decided it was healthy enough to be released into the wild as soon as possible.

Jo took the squirrel to a nearby park where she let it scuttle off up a tree and watched it disappear safely into the foliage.

Another nutty squirrel!

NAUGHTY

Lady was a naughty Staffordshire Bull Terrier brought in to see the vet after she went a bit mad with a box of chocolates.

She had eaten an entire box of assorted chocolates, including their foil wrappers.

Since then, she had still been eating well but Lady's owner was quite worried that the sweet wrappers might cause problems in Lady's tummy.

Vet Helen Kemp carefully felt Lady's stomach to check for blockages but all seemed normal. Helen told Lady's owner to bring her dog back if she became ill.

NAUGHTY LESSONS

The main reason dogs are naughty is because they have not received proper obedience and socialisation training. Your vet can give you tips on training and advise you about classes held locally.

Other reasons why your pet may develop bad behaviour include puberty, boredom, and lack of exercise.

Remember! Dogs need regular walks and play.

O is for...

Sacha's owner described the Boxer dog's worrying symptoms to vet Gabriel Haggard and Rolf Harris.

OPERATION

Sacha, the suspected 'gastroenteritis' case, needed surgery.

Often, a physical examination of a patient does not give the vet enough information to make a proper diagnosis.

In such cases, examining an animal under anaesthetic, and operating on it can be the next step...

Sacha, a three-year-old Boxer dog was brought into the RSPCA Harmsworth after vomiting and suffering from diarrhoea for several days.

Vet Gabriel Haggard examined Sacha and noted that she had a high temperature.

He also felt her stomach to check for signs of tenderness.

Gabriel suspected that Sacha had gastro-enteritis but needed to put Sacha under anaesthetic and examine her thoroughly in surgery to confirm his suspicions.

Once Sacha was unconscious in the operating theatre, the vet looked at her large intestine wall, but was unable to make a clear diagnosis.

Because of this, Gabriel also performed a biopsy, which would be sent off for testing in the laboratory.

The biopsy involved taking a small sample of tissue from Sacha's tummy, which would be examined by the lab to check for the presence of disease.

Without this biopsy, treating Sacha's illness successfully would be very difficult.

The vet would have to wait for the results of the biopsy before treating Sacha.

In the meantime, Sacha was admitted to the Harmsworth ward and given fluids to help rehydrate her, and hopefully lower her temperature.

When the biopsy results came back from the laboratory, they showed that Sacha had a condition called 'ulcerative colitis'.

Gabriel was able to prescribe a treatment for Sacha, who is now doing very well.

OSTRICH

When Rolf and the Animal Hospital team went to Australia, Rolf and flying vet Graham Stabler went to visit an ostrich farm as part of the vet's rounds.

They were called to the farm because one ostrich chick had died suddenly of a heart condition.

The chick's illness was caused by a vitamin E deficiency, so the vet had to examine the other chicks and give them all a vitamin supplement.

Each chick was examined. The vet listened to their chests for any signs of wheezing or rattling, before injecting them with a mixture of vitamins A, D, E, and C.

This injection would help counteract any vitamin deficiency. Graham also watched the chicks as they ran around to see if he could spot any problems with their leg movements.

Fortunately, all the chicks seemed fine.

Cane had more than just a sore throat, as vet Helen Kemp was startled to discover...

OUCH!

Cane's owner noticed that her dog had lost his bark and was bringing his food straight back up again whenever he tried to eat.

She thought her dog had swallowed something, which was causing the problem, but she wasn't sure what.

Vet Helen Kemp decided to anaesthetise Cane so she could take a closer look in his mouth. Immediately, she saw lots of cotton thread going down his throat.

The important question now was whether it was attached to a needle or not.

Vet Helen took two x-rays, one of Cane's throat and chest and one of his abdomen.

Both x-rays came up clear, so Helen set about removing the cotton.

Just as she began to remove the cotton, Helen had a nasty shock. There *was* a needle, and it was stuck right into Cane's tongue.

Helen had never seen anything quite like this before. No wonder Cane had seemed a little depressed.

Very carefully, the vet pulled out the needle and all the attached thread. Cane's tongue was not sore for too much longer.

OWL

Humans tend to come in contact with wild animals only when they are injured or very sick.

The rest of the time, their nature dictates that we might only get a glimpse of them from a distance.

One beautiful but sad example of a wild animal that the RSPCA staff came into contact with, was a male Tawny Owl which had been hit by a car travelling at 97 km/h.

The owl was brought into Harmsworth surgery to be checked over by the duty vet.

The owl was suffering from concussion, but otherwise had escaped with only one potentially serious injury.

During the accident, the owl had damaged its eye. The lens was bruised, which meant its sight was impaired.

As owls rely on their excellent vision for hunting, the owl would not be able to hunt and feed properly.

This meant he could not be released back into the wild as he would not be able to fend for himself.

The owl was transported from Harmsworth to the Eagle Heights Birds of Prey Centre to rehabilitate. Once there, the owl received specialist care and was observed to see if its eye improved.

Hopefully, the owl's eye will recover and he can be released back into the wild.

P is for... PARROT

Parrots are intelligent birds that can get easily bored if they do not live in a stimulating environment.

Freddy, a noisy parrot who was quite a character, had been to visit the Harmsworth vets a number of times.

On this occasion, Freddy's owner explained that Freddy had been pulling out a single, large feather every day for the past week.

He was not going bald, and was still eating well, but Freddy's owner was worried that something was wrong.

Vet Jeremy Stewart examined Freddy's feathers and noted that they were in good condition, despite his poor diet — his owner said he enjoyed eating fried eggs and spaghetti!

After a brief examination, the vet said that it was probably just a phase that Freddy was going through. Hopefully, he would grow out of it soon, but it wasn't a serious problem.

A blue and yellow macaw munches on a chilli fruit.

PLASTIC SURGERY

Animals will try and put almost anything in their mouths. Polystyrene is a common favourite, especially when it is part of the packaging of a food that a pet has a taste for.

Vet Jeremy Stewart was on duty at the RSPCA Harmsworth Animal Hospital when a loveable Old English Sheep Dog called Barnie was brought in by his anxious owner.

Barnie's owner explained to the vet that Barnie had eaten a polystyrene tray that had contained meat.

Barnie had not been sick, so it was obviously still in Barnie's tummy – somewhere!

The vet felt his stomach and abdomen. Barnie didn't seem to be in pain, but his tummy felt a bit 'gassy' which suggested that there was probably a problem of some kind.

Jeremy took an x-ray and the result was not as good as he had hoped. Barnie would need surgery to remove the plastic.

Barnie was anaesthetised before the operation began.

Jeremy removed the plastic pieces but also found some large, sharp pieces of bone which needed to be removed.

The operation was a success, but the vet warned his owners about allowing Barnie to eat bones.

He told them that dogs should never be allowed cooked bones, and that raw bones should only be given very rarely.

Ten days later, Barnie came back to have his stitches removed. He had made a full recovery.

PONIES

Ponies are small horses which are great fun but are also expensive and a lot of hard work. You should think very carefully before getting one as a pet.

- **Ponies need:** lots of space, exercise, mucking out daily, and regular grooming.
- **Ponies live for many years,** so buying a pony is a long-term commitment.
- **Don't forget,** there are many alternatives to buying a pony. There are riding schools and stables throughout the country.

The poor Jack Russell puppy whose tail was cruelly hacked off.

PUPPY TAIL

An RSPCA officer brought in a young Jack Russell for Vet Jeremy Stewart to look at. The dog had been handed into the police as a stray, but the puppy's tail looked as though it had been cut off with a knife and she had a nasty wound there.

Jeremy examined the young dog's tail. She had a large abscess at the base of her tail, which could be very serious if the infection spread up the spine.

Because the wound was so painful and the Jack Russell had been through an ordeal already, vet Jeremy did not want to operate unless it was really necessary.

He gave the puppy some antibiotics which would hopefully reduce the swelling and help contain the infection.

However, after a few days, the tail was nastily infected and Jeremy was forced to operate.

When the puppy was under anaesthetic, Jeremy could see that some of the tailbone itself was exposed.

The bone would have to be covered with skin for the tail to have a chance to heal.

Jeremy cut a tiny piece more of the bone off and then pulled the healthy skin tissue and stitched it carefully over the tail bone.

Luckily for the puppy, she had recovered enough in just two days for her to go to a re-homing centre.

After a short time there, her tail was healing very well and she was friendly and lively – not at all like the sorry dog that had been brought into the RSPCA Harmsworth.

q is for...

QUACKERS

Two RSPCA ambulance drivers were called out to a London pond. The park warden there was worried about the condition of a mallard and a young Canadian goose.

The warden thought they had been attacked by some local children. He also had not seen either bird fly. The birds were young, but they should still have learnt to fly by now, so he knew something must be wrong.

The warden helped the RSPCA officers to chase and capture the birds. They decided to spread out with nets, but it was still a tough job.

They had just caught the goose when disaster struck. The mallard swam to a part of the pond that had dense plant life, and became trapped under weeds, unable to breathe.

The warden strode into the water and got to the duck just in time.

When the RSPCA officers arrived back at the Harmsworth, vet Jeremy Stewart examined the birds in turn.

The goose was very thin and small for its age, its wings were not broken, but in a poor state.

Similarly, the mallard had no broken bones but was significantly underweight.

Jeremy said the birds were probably just very badly traumatised after the children had attacked them, resulting in their appetite loss and current state of malnutrition. It was malnutrition that had prevented the birds from flying.

The pair were taken to the nearby Egham Swan Sanctuary where they were soon nursed back to health.

Within a week, both birds had put on weight and made excellent progress.

Vet Jeremy Stewart examines the goose for broken bones.

The police and the RSPCA were amazed to find this little chap locked in an abandoned car boot.

RESCUE

RSPCA Inspector Gary Lucas received a call about a dog reported to have been locked inside the boot of a parked car.

When he arrived, Gary found the car in question and listened for any signs of life.

The inspector could not hear anything, and was unsure whether there was an animal inside after all.

When he contacted the police, Gary learned that there was no record of the car's owner.

Because the car had been abandoned, the police were allowed to help Gary prise open the car boot.

When he opened the car boot, the officer was horrified to find a dog inside. It had been locked in without food or water, but seemed to be unaffected by its ordeal.

Just to make sure the dog was in good health, the RSPCA inspector took it to the Putney Animal Hospital where chief vet Tessa Bailey examined it.

Tessa examined the dog, which she thought was aged between four and six years. The dog seemed to have been well fed until recently and was physically fit.

After giving it some food and water, the dog was transferred to a kennel.

Luckily, the dog was spotted on television and was reunited with its owners who had been frantic.

Not only had their car been stolen but their beloved dog had gone missing too. Now that's what we call a rescue!

r is for...

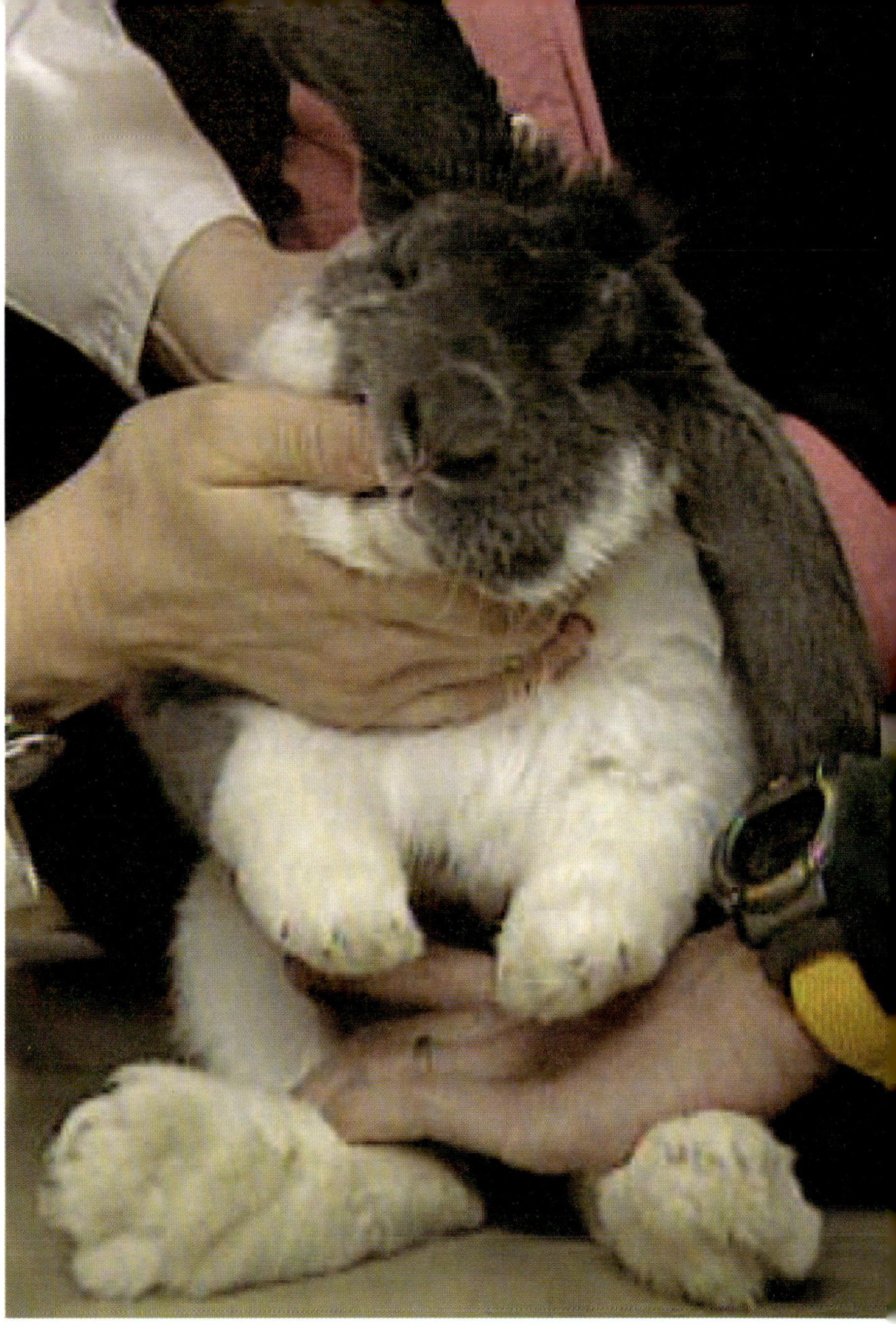

It took a team effort to hold Genie down while vet Liz Forbes examined him.

RABBIT

Genie, a French lop-eared rabbit, was brought into the Putney Animal Hospital surgery to see vet Liz Forbes. Over the past week, Genie had become very aggressive.

The rabbit was not only scratching and kicking but had even bitten his owner's chin.

Liz examined Genie briefly, but already had a good idea what might be causing the increase in Genie's aggressive behaviour.

Apparently, Genie had become more aggressive because he was maturing and would soon reach puberty.

In order to stop Genie from becoming even more hostile, Liz said that Genie should be castrated.

Many pet owners are concerned about this procedure, but vet Liz explained that it is, in fact, a straightforward and virtually painless operation.

The operation is designed to lower the hormonal levels, returning the rabbit to its usual friendly self.

Genie's owner agreed to the operation, and sure enough, Genie was soon back to his old friendly self.

Dave, Grizz and his feral friend, who is never far away... especially when food is around!

RESCUE & REHABILITATION

In the Animal Hospital Goes West series, Rolf went to meet a man called Dave Siddon who was devoted to rescuing and caring for Grizzly Bears.

Dave took Rolf to meet Grizz, his favourite rescued bear, who had been hit by a train as a cub and lost an eye. Grizz had been living in Dave's bear sanctuary ever since.

Dave explained that Grizz was relatively friendly, but weighing in at around 317.5 kg, he was not to be taken lightly!

However, Grizz was a bit of a softie – his best friend was a wild cat that had wandered into Grizz's enclosure about a year ago. The pair had been virtually inseparable ever since.

Although Grizz would never live outside captivity, Dave told Rolf that he also had about 15 rescued bears, whose chances were better.

Hopefully, after a little rehabilitation, these bears would all be able to be released back into the wild.

One of Dave's rescued bears sharpens his claws on a tree.

RSPCA

The Royal Society for the Prevention of Cruelty to Animals, RSPCA, was set up in 1824.

The RSPCA is the world's oldest and largest charity devoted to animal welfare.

Based in England and Wales, the RSPCA has a team of around 320 inspectors.

The RSPCA has animal hospitals across the country, three of which deal especially with wildlife.

RE-HOMING RABBITS

Around six stray rabbits are brought into the Harmsworth surgery every week.

After any treatment they might need, they are taken to the RSPCA Southridge Animal Centre in Hertfordshire for re-homing.

Unfortunately, rabbits can be unpopular and abused pets. This is because they are often given to children who get bored with looking after them. All too often, the rabbits are found as strays because they are let out of their cages.

The poor rabbits make easy prey for cats and dogs and are often brought to the hospital's veterinary staff in poor condition.

P.J. gives Rolf her seal of approval!

And… action!

At rehearsals: P.J. and his trainer Scott.

S is for… SEA LIONS

During the Animal Hospital Goes West series, Rolf went to watch the American Humane Association (AHA), at work…

The AHA is devoted to the welfare of all animals used in films.

The Animal Hospital team visited a film set where an AHA member was inspecting some sea lions to check that these animal stars were treated correctly.

Scott, the trainer of the sea lions, was asked a number of questions about the animals' welfare, such as how long were the rest periods between filming.

During the inspection of the sea lions and their habitat, Rolf was fortunate enough to get to meet quite a few of the playful characters.

One of the sea lions, P.J., was a three-year-old female who was very friendly and well-trained.

Scott explained that P.J. really enjoyed performing tricks, and just to prove how happy she was in the limelight, she gave Rolf a big kiss!

STUCK!

While cats are renowned for being very agile creatures, they also tend to get stuck in all sorts of places. Lewis was no exception.

The RSPCA were called when Lewis' owner was worried. She said that her cat had been stuck on a roof overnight and seemed distressed as a result.

The cat's owner explained that Lewis had been wailing all night, and there had been no sign of him attempting to climb back down.

The RSPCA officer decided to enlist the help of the local fire brigade.

They came to Lewis' aid with a ladder long enough to reach him on the roof.

Just as the fireman climbed up to where Lewis was, the cat got scared and hid behind a chimney stack.

The fireman didn't give up though and after some coaxing, he managed to bring Lewis safely back down to earth to a very happy and relieved owner.

Tiddles on the roof! Lewis was stuck on a roof for hours, but when a fireman tried to help him down, he nervously retreated to a chimney stack.

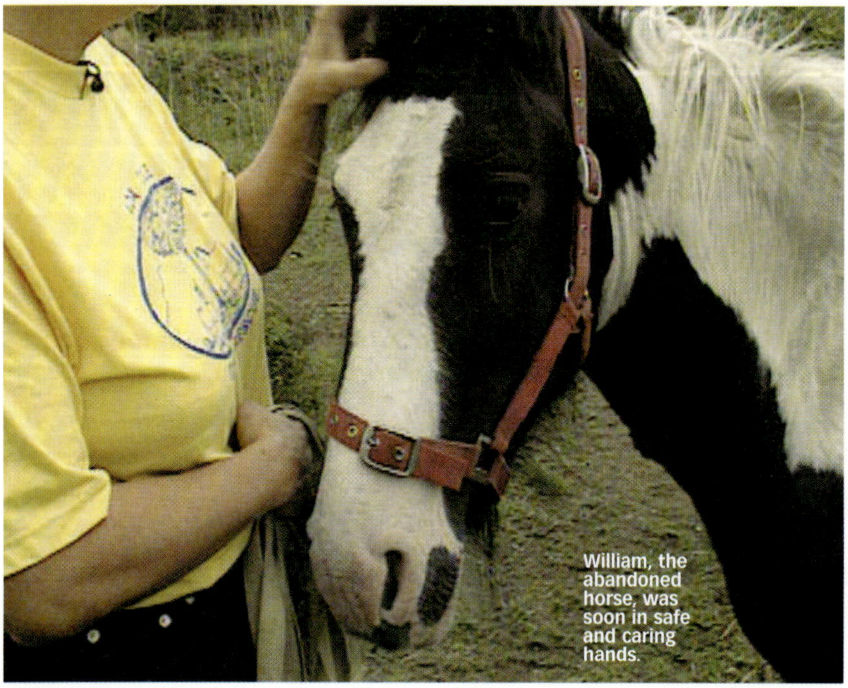

William, the abandoned horse, was soon in safe and caring hands.

STRAY

RSPCA Inspector John Bowe was called when workmen spotted a stray horse, abandoned in a field near a busy road.

The workmen had set up a makeshift water trough by the edge of the field, to give the horse a daily fresh water source.

Several weeks on, there was still no sign of an owner. As there was no obvious way to get into the field, the RSPCA needed the police's permission to cut a hole in the fence, large enough to coax the horse through.

The vet examined the stallion and found an infection on one of his forelegs, which a skin scrape later revealed was due to a mite infestation.

The vet prescribed an injection to kill the mites and antibiotics for the infection.

After his analysis, the horse was taken to rescue stables in Essex where he was kept in isolation until his skin problem had healed properly.

The stray, now called William, had made good progress.

William went on to receive basic training as he needed to be broken in before he could be re-homed.

Hey! Where's the pond?!

Home: the swan is greeted by his family.

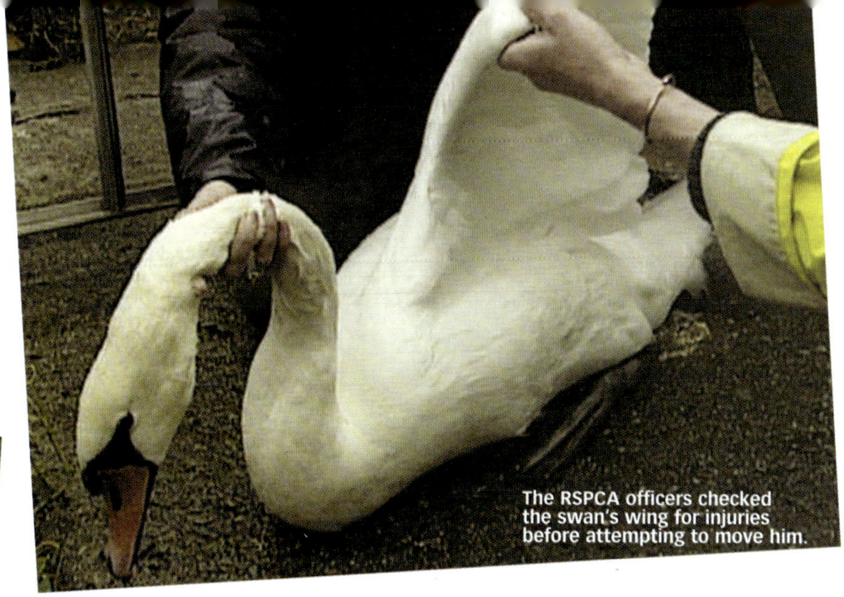

The RSPCA officers checked the swan's wing for injuries before attempting to move him.

SWAN

Two RSPCA ambulance drivers were called to the rescue of a swan which had crash-landed in a garden on a very windy day.

The swan could walk without difficulty but it had not attempted to fly off again. This was why the garden's owner thought the swan might require some help.

The RSPCA officers told the man that his house was underneath a popular flight path for migrating swans, and close to a lake where they often landed.

The officers looked at the swan but found it was uninjured. The reason he had not flown away was because swans require a long run-up to be able to take off.

The RSPCA officers transported the young male swan back to the nearby lake believing this to be his most probable destination, and likely to be home.

When they arrived at the lake, they saw a female swan with her offspring who they suspected were the missing family of the male swan.

Very carefully they released the swan on to the lake to see if he would rejoin them. To their satisfaction, his family immediately swam over to meet him.

SCARED!

Snakes are among the most feared creatures in the world and are generally considered not to make good pets. Apart from having very specialist needs, some breeds of snake are poisonous or deadly.

It is part of the RSPCA officers' service to protect these exotic animals, whether they are snake-lovers or not.

When an RSPCA driver called Barbara received a call from a lady one morning, she was dreading what she would find at the scene. Barbara was absolutely terrified of snakes, and frankly would rather have not received the call!

The lady had reported finding a skinny, stray snake in the middle of the road. With only this information, Barbara had no idea how dangerous the snake was. It might be angry and vicious as a result of its ordeal.

There was also a chance it could be extremely poisonous or even deadly. Luckily, when Barbara arrived on the scene, the cold weather had made the snake quite docile.

The snake had been lying in the road all morning so it was probably getting hungry.

Barbara could not identify the snake initially, which meant she still didn't know whether the snake was poisonous or not. She therefore took all the necessary precautions to prevent getting bitten while handling the snake.

The next step would be for a vet to check the snake's condition. Then it could be found a new home, with a more responsible owner.

A harmless variety of the Mexican red-kneed bird-eating spider.

SPIDER

How well do you know your arachnids? Although we see spiders every day, most people don't know much about them.

After finding an unusual-looking spider in her home, the occupant thought she had better bring it to Harmsworth to be identified by the experts.

A duty nurse tried to identify the specimen. The woman said she thought the spider might be an unusual species because it looked so big and had quite distinct markings.

The nurse believed the spider might be a common garden spider, but just to be sure, they went to see an expert at London Zoo.

The arachnid specialist soon confirmed that the woman's spider was in fact a common garden spider, but took the opportunity to show her some of the rarer spiders kept at the zoo.

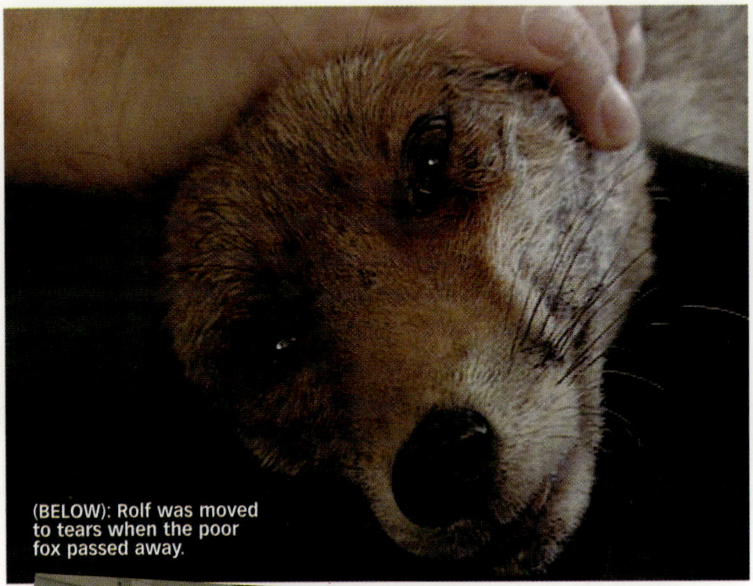

(BELOW): Rolf was moved to tears when the poor fox passed away.

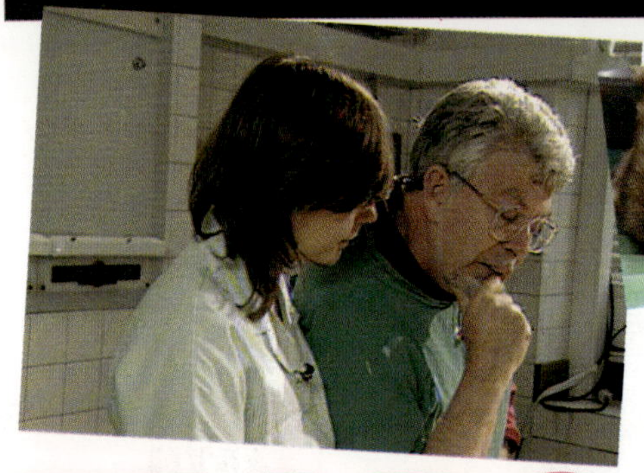

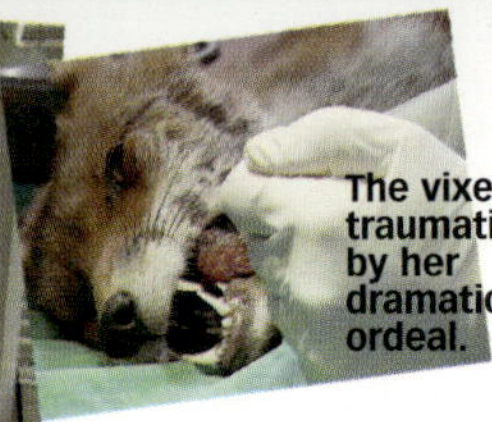

The vixen was traumatised by her dramatic ordeal.

TEARS

Sometimes, the effort and will of the veterinary staff at RSPCA Harmsworth and Putney Animal Hospitals is not enough to save an animal's life.

It is always sad when an animal brought into clinic dies.

However, the number of success stories that leave the hospitals helps to counter such upsetting moments.

Vet Helen Kemp was the vet on duty at the RSPCA Putney Animal Hospital when an RSPCA inspector brought in a very unwell fox.

The fox had got her head stuck in some fence railings.

She had been there for quite a while before an RSPCA inspector and the policeman were called and managed to prise the bars apart to rescue her.

Once at Putney, the fox was sedated immediately so the vet could have a proper look at her, which also helped to ease her fear of human contact. The fox was put on to a drip to try and rehydrate her, and help combat shock.

When the fox got stuck in between the railings, she had panicked and chewed through her tongue. She also had a large twig stuck across the roof of her inflamed mouth.

Helen cleaned and stitched up the fox but her tongue would never be normal.

Suddenly, the nurse told the vet that the fox had stopped breathing, but her heartbeat was still strong.

She immediately began to ventilate the fox manually, but unfortunately the fox's heart stopped beating.

It was a tense moment, Helen had to act fast. She immediately injected the fox with adrenaline directly into the heart to try and start it again.

Sadly, the heart did not respond. The accident and operation had been all too much of a shock for the fox.

Everyone was upset and poor Rolf couldn't fight back the tears on this occasion.

TEARY-EYED

Rabbits often have problems with their eyes, usually caused by blockages within the tear ducts.

A rabbit called William came to the surgery regularly to have his tear ducts flushed. Without the treatment, he would develop very watery, teary eyes due to his tear duct becoming infected.

The vet used eye drops containing local anaesthetic to numb the rabbit's eyes.

She then carefully used a narrow tube called a 'cannula' to clean his tear ducts.

Fluid was pushed along William's tear ducts to force out any blockages.

The fluid came out of the rabbit's nose, and although it looked like a bizarre procedure, the vet explained that it was a painless and simple procedure that would give William considerable relief. William's eyes were clear once again.

William: bright-eyed and bushy-tailed once more.

t is for...

The tortoise was weighed so the vet could calculate the exact amount of anaesthetic required.

TORTOISE

One of the stops on the Animal Hospital Goes West tour was at the West Los Angeles Hospital, a high tech hospital for animals.

Rolf met Dr Doug Madder, a vet who specialised in reptiles, who was treating a large Californian Desert Tortoise with a painful problem.

The vet explained that the tortoise's owner had noticed that the animal was not urinating.

When Dr Madder examined the tortoise, an x-ray revealed that the tortoise had two huge bladder stones.

Dr Madder would have to operate to remove the painful stones, so he invited Rolf to watch.

The tortoise was given a tranquilliser and prepared for the operation by using a small toothbrush to scrub the shell.

The first step of the operation was to drill through the tough shell. Once completed, Dr Madder quickly located the stones.

Using a teaspoon, the vet very carefully removed the stones. Incredibly, these bladder stones were the same size as tennis balls!

With the stones removed, the vet sewed the tortoise up and replaced the shell.

The tortoise was around 40 to 50 years old. Hopefully she would live for that many years again.

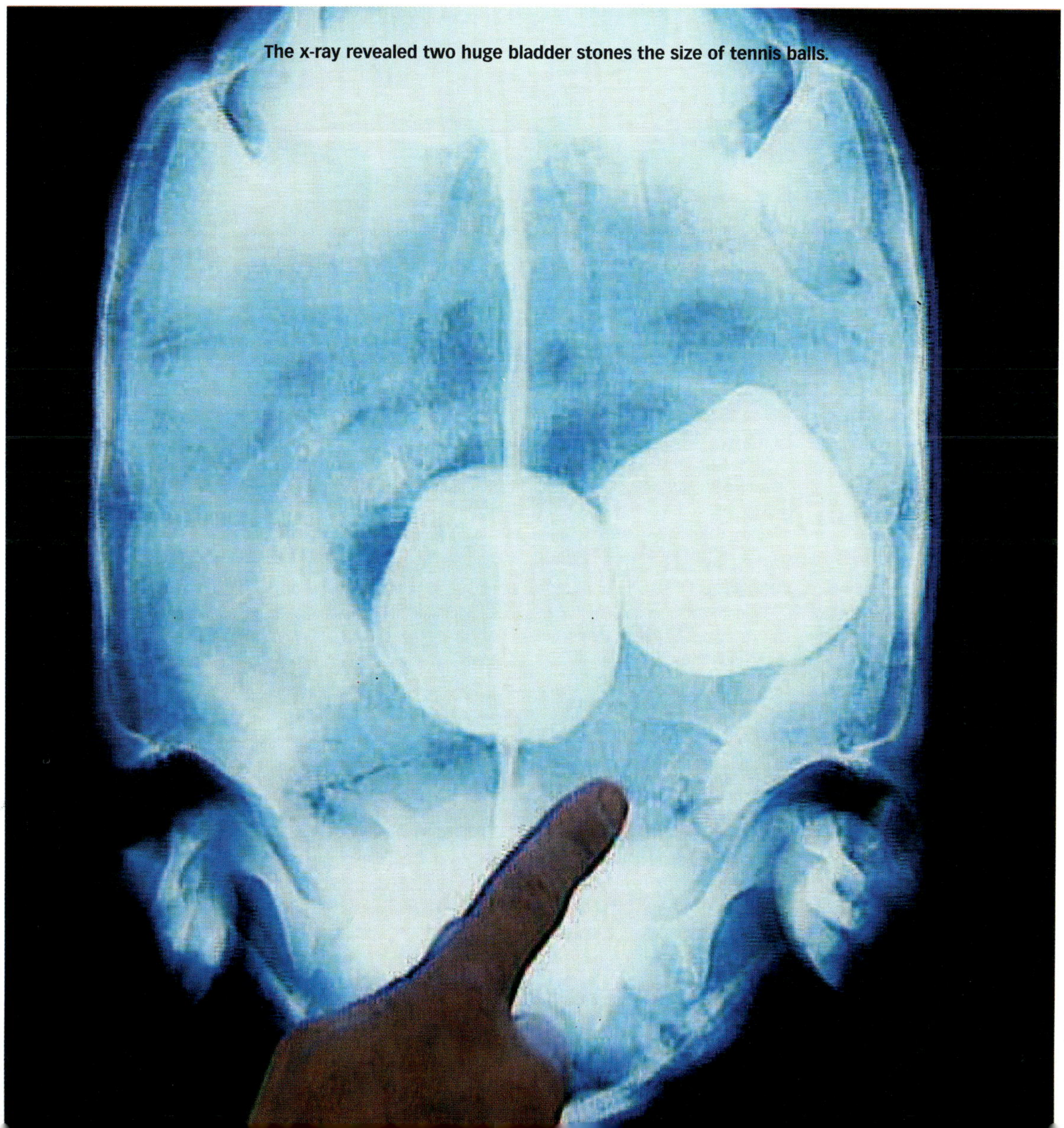

The x-ray revealed two huge bladder stones the size of tennis balls.

TEETH

The teeth of rabbits and rodents grow continuously.

This is why it is important for them to have plenty of things to gnaw on, thus ensuring that your pet can keep its teeth properly filed down.

Most other pets have teeth that grow in the same way as yours do. But there's an important difference...

Whereas we can brush our teeth regularly and pay visits to the dentist for a check up, animals do not tend to have such a good dental hygiene routine!

TERMINATOR'S TEETH...

It is amazing how many dental problems the RSPCA Animal Hospital vets have to treat. This is partly because pets cannot brush their teeth to protect against tooth decay and gum disease.

Some animals have teeth that will keep on growing if they are not worn down or trimmed regularly.

A hamster called Terminator had teeth problems when chief vet David Grant saw him.

His owner explained that the hamster was only eating on one side of his mouth. This was odd, as Terminator normally ate anything, anytime, and was more than happy to do so.

David examined Terminator's mouth, and noted it was tender on one side. The teeth were very long and desperately needed clipping.

Once David had done this, the hamster would soon be munching happily once more!

U is for...

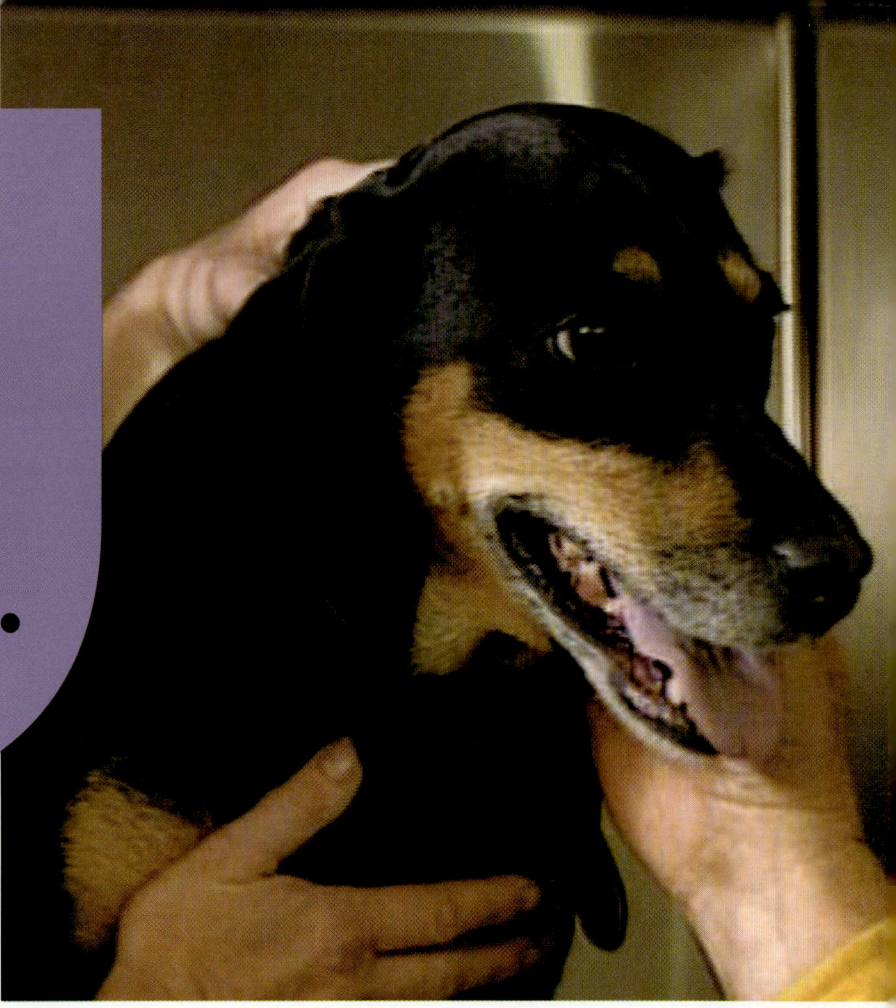

Cindy, who made a full recovery after her bladder stone operation.

UNHAPPY ENDING

Sometimes a pet that comes into the veterinary surgery wins the affection of everyone there, as was the case with Summer, a puppy.

Summer was only nine months old when her owner brought her into clinic.

For about a week, Summer was sick every time she tried to eat and she also made a peculiar snoring noise when she breathed.

After listening to Summer's chest, the vet took an x-ray of her lungs and wind-pipe and found that Summer's airway was very narrow. There was also fluid on Summer's lungs, which had caused her to make the unusual breathing sounds.

Summer was in very bad condition and needed to be admitted to the intensive care ward where she was tube-fed to try and rebuild her strength.

Poor Summer was so ill that the vet advised the puppy's owner to seriously consider the option of putting Summer to sleep. There was no guarantee Summer would survive, even if she had surgery.

Summer was then given a series of X-rays, which showed her food pipe was so swollen that it made her sick every time she ate.

Obviously Summer was unable to survive without food. Tragically, the problem could not be fixed, and Summer had to be put to sleep. There was nothing else anyone could do for the poor puppy.

UNBELIEVABLE!

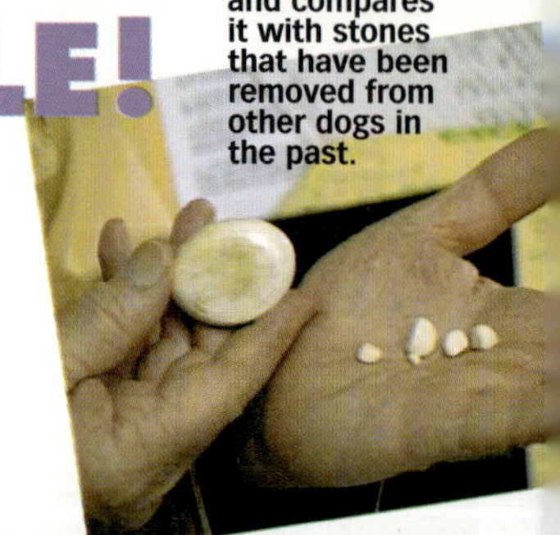

Rolf holds up Cindy's stone and compares it with stones that have been removed from other dogs in the past.

There is not a lot that surprises the staff at the RSPCA Animal Hospitals, simply because over the years, they have seen some of the strangest pets and the most bizarre ailments.

However, the case of Cindy the dog left vet Bairbre O' Malley amazed.

Cindy's symptoms were indicative of cystitis, a urinary infection that can be treated with antibiotics.

However, after a course of antibiotics there was still quite a lot of blood in Cindy's urine. Even worse was the lump present in Cindy's abdomen.

Bairbre suspected that Cindy might have a tumour in her bladder, but the only way to be sure was to take x-rays, and then remove it.

Bairbre soon realised that what she thought was a tumour, was in fact a huge bladder stone that needed to be removed.

Two hours later, with Cindy safely anaesthetised, Bairbre managed to remove the stone.

She was totally stunned to find Cindy's stone was the size of a ping pong ball — a huge stone to find in a dog!

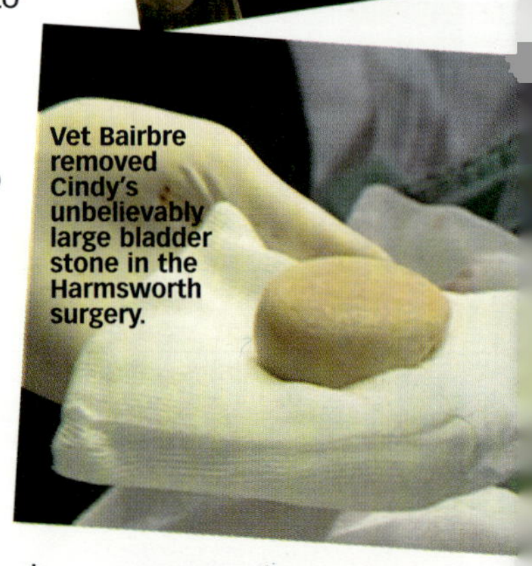

Vet Bairbre removed Cindy's unbelievably large bladder stone in the Harmsworth surgery.

After just two weeks of rest at home, Cindy was ready to return to RSPCA Harmsworth to have her stitches removed.

Bairbre said Cindy had made incredible progress. In fact, she commented that Cindy was now far bubblier and full of beans. Much better than being full of stones!

Rolf in Tessa Bailey's house, getting to know her latest adoptees.

V is for... VETS AND THEIR PETS

The dedication to animals of the staff at the RSPCA Animal Hospitals does not stop when they leave work.

TESSA'S MENAGERIE

Putney's chief vet Tessa Bailey has pets in every room of her house!

When the Animal Hospital team were invited to have a look at her pets, they were amazed to find twenty-four animals in her house to greet them.

Over the years, vet Tessa and her husband have adopted many abandoned pets. She now has pets in every room, including an aviary in her bathroom.

Each pet has its own particular story. Among the birds in Tessa's aviary is a pair of finches who had been left at a supermarket, in a cardboard box.

Tessa also has many cats, dogs, rabbits and birds with permanent injures or deformities, making them very difficult to re-home. Thankfully, Tessa was on hand to adopt them, and give these animals somewhere to call home.

When the Animal Hospital team visited Tessa's house, they found her hand-rearing some orphaned kittens.

Tessa explained that because the kittens needed to be fed every two hours, she had to take them to work with her. Now, how about that for dedication?

VETS AND THEIR PETS

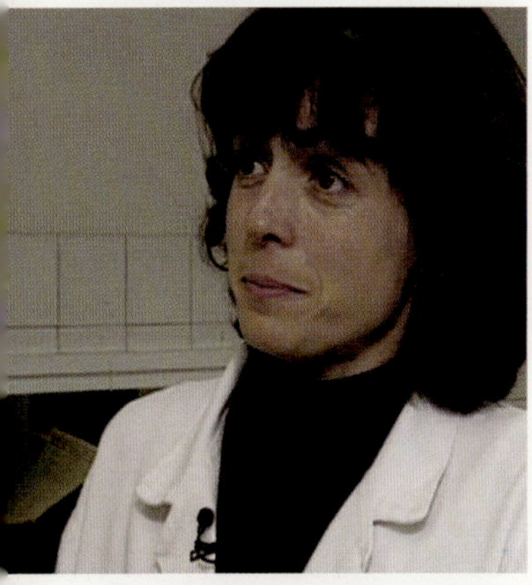

HELEN AND HER RABBIT CALLED DIGGER

Vet Helen Kemp is very devoted to her pet rabbit Digger. She adopted him from a re-homing centre about four years ago.

Helen had visited the re-homing centre with no intention of taking home one of its residents, but simply couldn't resist Digger.

Digger fitted into Helen's life very quickly, becoming a lively member of the Kemp household.

One day, however, the moment every pet-owner dreads arrived — Digger became ill. An anxious Helen knew that she would have to operate.

Digger had developed an abscess in his cheek. Helen needed to give him an anaesthetic and cut out the abscess. Helen admitted that she was terrified.

She was hopeful that the infection had not spread to the jawbone, which would have been very serious.

The abscess did, in fact, go a lot deeper than Helen had first suspected but she was able to remove the abscess in one piece.

She stitched up the wound and when Digger awoke, he looked as though he was fairly comfortable.

The next day, Helen was still very anxious when she went to check on Digger's progress. She gave him a thorough check-up and found he had made enough progess through the night that he was able go home. What a relief!

VETS IN THE SURGERY

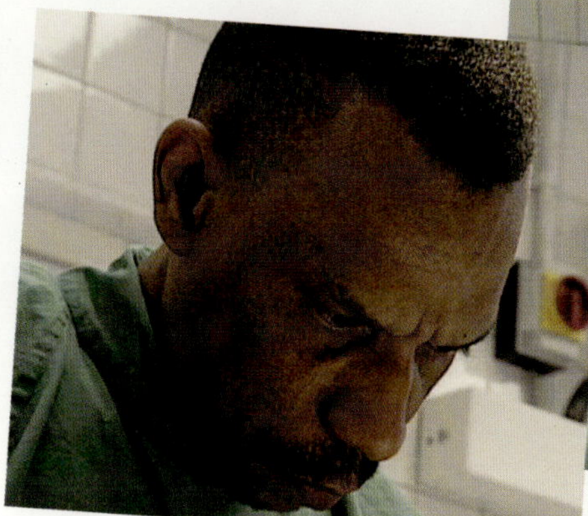

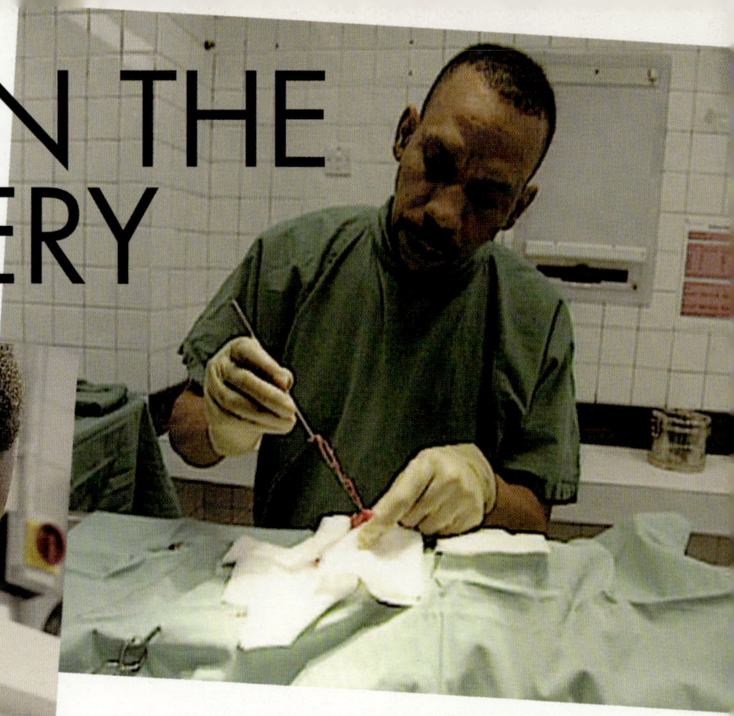

(Above): Vet Stan McCasky concentrates on the tricky task at hand. **Moments later.**. Eureka! Stan very carefully removes cotton swallowed by a cat

(Above): Remember Freddy, the spaghetti-eating parrot? Vet Jeremy Stewart does!

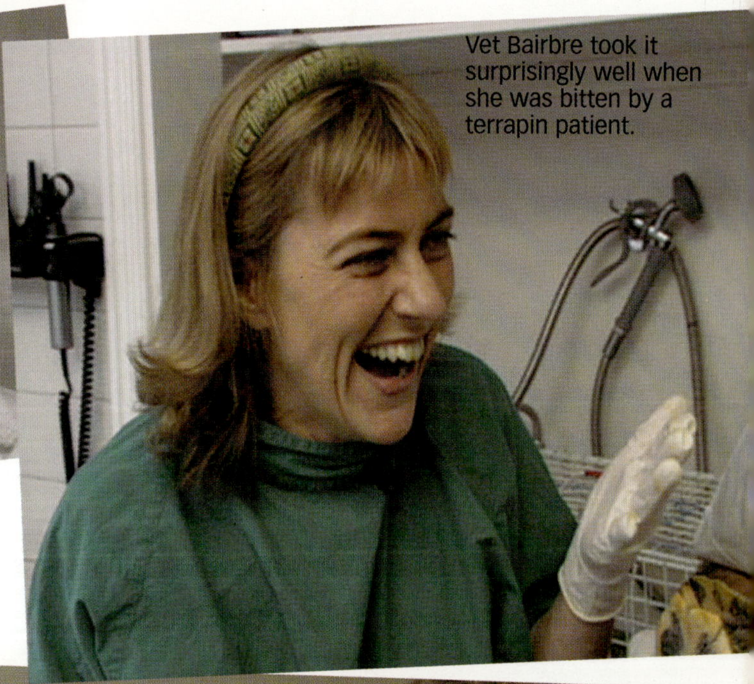

Vet Bairbre took it surprisingly well when she was bitten by a terrapin patient.

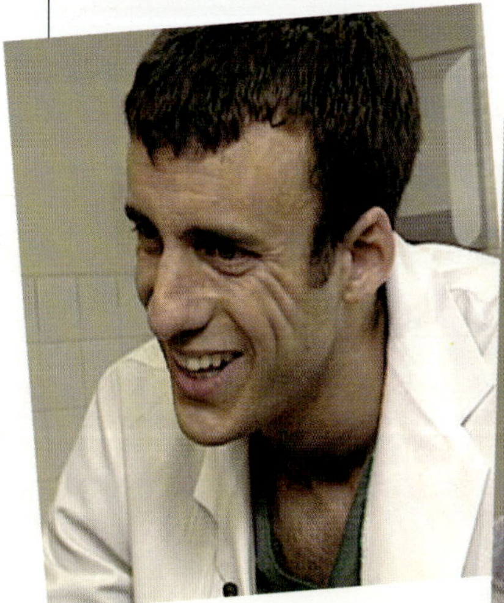

(Above): Vet Gabriel Haggard shares a joke with a patient's owner.

(Right): RSPCA Harmsworth's chief vet David Grant explains the finer points of 'paw lick' to a dog's owner.

W is for... WILDLIFE

In recent years, some wildlife species have become almost as common in towns as they are in the countryside. However, this doesn't mean that they are any less 'wild' in nature.

Remember....
Many wild animals and birds die from shock alone, even from a loud or sudden noise, so handling a wild animal is extremely hazardous.

If you have serious reason to believe a wild animal is in trouble, call the RSPCA or a nearby vet who will tell you exactly what to do.

Keiko gets a well-earned snack.

WHALE

When the Animal Hospital team were touring California, they caught up with a famous film star!

They met Keiko the killer whale — star of *Free Willy*, the hit children's movie.

Rolf was introduced to Keiko's keepers who explained that Keiko was around 19 years old and had never lived in the wild with other Orca whales.

They told Rolf that before he could be released into the wild, he would need to learn to hunt properly and socialise with other whales.

Keiko's trainers also aimed to build up Keiko's muscles, increase his body mass and, hopefully, strengthen his immune system.

He has already made great progress since the Animal Hospital team's visit, and has been transferred away from the public eye to Iceland. Here, his trainers are now teaching Keiko to hunt successfully.

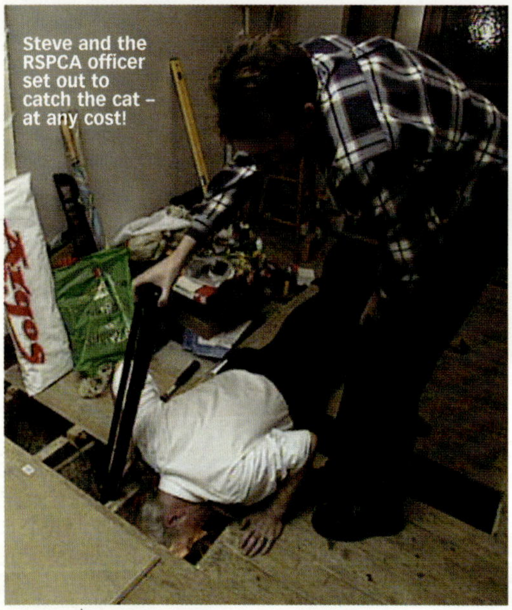
Steve and the RSPCA officer set out to catch the cat – at any cost!

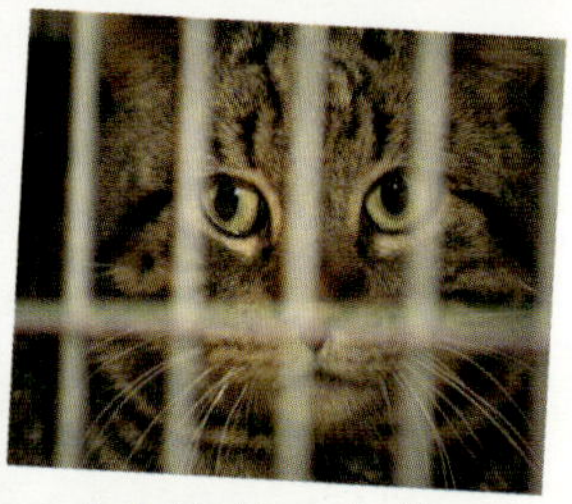
Safe behind bars (rather than under floorboards).

WILD GOOSE CHASE

It's not always easy for the RSPCA to get their hands on the animals they're trying to help. Take this case:

An RSPCA inspector was called out by a man who said that he had a cat stuck beneath the floor-boards of his house.

He had already taken up some of the floorboards in an attempt to free the cat, but without any luck so far.

The inspector asked if he could take up some more floorboards, but each time he caught a glimpse of the cat, it got scared and ran off.

After an hour of searching and ripping up floorboards, the RSPCA inspector had still not managed to coax the cat out.

He decided to use Plan B instead! He used food as a bait, and left it overnight.

The next morning, the house owner called the RSPCA again to report that the cat had taken the bait during the night. They had been able to catch the cat!

It was then taken to the RSPCA Putney Hospital for a thorough check-up.

Apart from being a little thin, the cat did not seem too upset by its ordeal and was sent to a re-homing centre.

WAX

A cat was brought in to see chief vet David Grant after the owner noticed the cat was shaking her head.

David examined the cat's ear and noticed that she had a lot of wax built up in there. He prescribed some special ear drops.

But David was much more worried about the size of the cat than about her ear! She was absolutely huge and as a result, she could no longer groom herself properly.

David said that it was imperative that the cat lost weight.The owner promised to reduce her cat's rations.

The fox made good progress.

WILD

Wild animals usually avoid human contact at all costs, so when an RSPCA officer was called to help an injured fox, he expected to have quite a job trying to catch the fox.

Eventually he managed to corner the fox and get her to run into a box.

Bairbre O'Malley was on duty at the RSPCA Harmsworth Hospital and was told about the case.

When vet Bairbre examined the fox, she saw that the skin on the vixen's neck was infected.

Bairbre said she would bathe the fox and give her an injection against mange. To help stop the infection from spreading, the fox also received a course of antibiotics and daily bathing until she recovered.

The fox was still weak but gradually began to respond to the treatment.

After chief vet David Grant had re-examined her, he was able to give the fox the 'all-clear'. She was taken to HydeStyle Wildlife Hospital, where she could complete her recovery.

X is for...

X-RAYS

X-rays can prove vital when detecting what is wrong with a pet and can sometimes save the animal's life. Over the years, the RSPCA Animal Hospital vets have been surprised at what turns up on x-rays — take a look at this example!

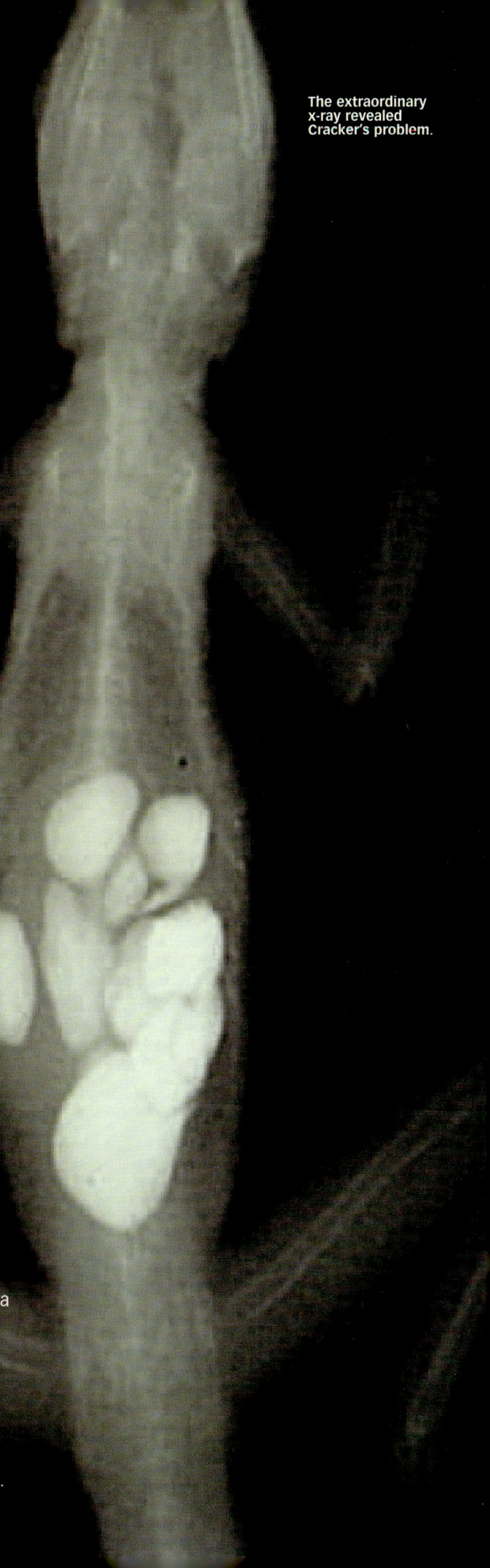

The extraordinary x-ray revealed Cracker's problem.

CRACKER'S X-RAY

Cracker was a pet water dragon who had not been eating and drinking much.

Cracker's owners told the vet that they had bought him four weeks ago and had been taking good care of him, but he had been losing weight.

Vet Helen Kemp examined Cracker. His mouth was clean and pink, which is a sign of good health, but he seemed to be a little dehydrated.

A healthy reptile's skin is normally quite tight, but Cracker's was slightly wrinkly when the vet pulled it gently.

Helen decided to carry out an x-ray to check the water dragon's calcium status.

The x-ray showed very clearly that Cracker had a marked calcium deficiency. His bones were very faint and thin.

To Helen's surprise, another thing the x-ray showed was that Cracker had been eating stones that had now become trapped in his abdomen.

Helen told Cracker's owners that he had eaten the stones in order to increase his calcium levels.

The vet was amazed. She had never seen anything like it, especially because the stones were so large.

Cracker was given some fluids to rehydrate him via a stomach tube. Mixed with the fluids was a laxative, to help Cracker pass the trapped stones.

A few days later, Cracker was able to pass a number of the stones. He had also been receiving some calcium injections to help improve his physical strength.

Once Cracker began drinking on his own, he seemed a lot livelier, and a second x-ray showed that only one stone was left.

Eventually, he managed to pass the final stone and the extra calcium injections helped to build up his bones and strength.

His owners were delighted.

The stones in question.

Y is for... YES!

Poor old Sky was feeling blue.

Sky was a beautiful female puppy who stole the hearts of all the Harmsworth staff when she made her first visit to the vet.

For such a young puppy, Sky was seriously ill. Everyone hoped that her life could be saved.

Sky's owner explained that he had bought her from a friend's litter. When he got her home, she seemed healthy.

However, within days, she had started to vomit and had diarrhoea. The owner tried Sky on different food but she remained sick. More worrying was the fact Sky had blood in her faeces.

Vet Jeremy asked Sky's owner some questions about Sky's background that might help him rule out certain illnesses.

Unfortunately, Sky's owner had not seen the condition of her mother, father or any of the other puppies from the litter.

He had no idea whether Sky's mother had been vaccinated against any potentially fatal illnesses.

This meant that Sky might not be immune to certain diseases.

Jeremy examined the puppy and found that she was seriously dehydrated, indicated by her skin 'tenting' when pulled gently.

Jeremy explained that Sky would go straight on a drip, to get some fluids directly into her blood system.

Sky was running a temperature and, because Jeremy was worried that she might have the contagious parvovirus, he put her on the isolation ward.

Luckily, Sky made a complete recovery. But her case illustrates just how essential vaccinations are.

The calves were upset when they saw their mother fall and went to see what was wrong.

YAK YAK YAK!

When a female yak at Whipsnade needed to have her hooves trimmed, keepers were faced with the daunting task of separating her from the rest of the herd.

Yaks can be dangerous, because their behaviour is unpredictable. It would take a team effort to ensure that the vet could carry out his work.

Once inside the yak enclosure, the vet had to get close enough to the yak to shoot a tranquiliser dart at her.

The tranquiliser took between five and ten minutes to take effect. As soon as the yak went down, keepers in cars herded away the other yaks.

They had to be particularly careful with the tranquilised yak's two young calves, who were rather distressed.

The yak's hooves were badly overgrown so it was well worth the team effort.

Once the hooves were in good order again, the yak was soon back on her feet and re-united with her two affectionate calves.

Z is for...

ZOO

Viewers of Animal Hospital are familiar with domestic pets. But, in the Animal Hospital on the Hoof series, we got a chance to learn about the more unusual animals and birds when we visited them at their home at London Zoo's sister wildlife park, Whipsnade Wild Animal Park.

Whipsnade is home to a variety of wild animals, many of which are endangered species.

The animals are able to live in relative freedom, roaming about in the park's large outdoor enclosure.

As well as being home to elephants, cheetahs, rhinoceroses, lions, giraffes and other wild animals, Whipsnade is a park for rare and unusual species of animal. For example, the park has one of the largest collections of Chinese Water Deer outside China.

Throughout the Animal Hospital on the Hoof series, the Animal Hospital team watched the vets and keepers hard at work in the wildlife park.

The case of the expectant Swamp Deer mother fascinated thousands of viewers. The deer collapsed and the vet had to perform a dramatic caesarean.

Fortunately, the baby Swamp Deer survived its exciting entry into the world and the Animal Hospital team were able to follow her progress as she was carefully hand-reared .

Then there was Burt, an orphaned vulture who was taught to fly by his keeper while the Animal Hospital team were there.

Burt's flying lessons ended in an incredible sky-high flight from a hot air balloon.

By following the vets and keepers, Animal Hospital was able to gain an insight into the importance of the work done there, and also into the care and dedication to the animals living in the Whipsnade Park.

Kangaroos at play.

Rolf takes a break near the flamingos.

A rare Chinese Water Deer.

Penguins at Whipsnade Wild Animal Park.

ZOONOSES

Zoonoses are diseases that can be transferred from animals to other animals, and also to humans, particularly children.

Fortunately, these are extremely rare, one of the most deadly being rabies, which is controlled in the UK by very strict quarantine laws.

More common are ringworm and sarcoptic mange, which should be treated by your vet as soon as possible.

Another type of zoonosis is a disease called 'toxoplasmosis', which can even cause defects in unborn children if a pregnant mother becomes infected with the parasite.

Toxoplasmosis affects many animals but is most common in cats. This is why you should always wash your hands after stroking any pet.

RSPCA

RSPCA Headquarters, Causeway, Horsham, West Sussex RH12 1HG

To report an animal in distress, please telephone the RSPCA's national cruelty and advice line:

Tel: 0870 55 55 999

Your call may be recorded for operational purposes.